STATISTICS DIRECTORATE

AF791100

MAIN ECONOMIC INDICATORS

Sources and Methods

INTEREST RATES AND SHARE PRICES

DECEMBER 1997

ORGANISATION FOR ECONOMIC CO-OPERATION AND DEVELOPMENT

ORGANISATION FOR ECONOMIC CO-OPERATION AND DEVELOPMENT

Pursuant to Article 1 of the Convention signed in Paris on 14th December 1960, and which came into force on 30th September 1961, the Organisation for Economic Co-operation and Development (OECD) shall promote policies designed:

- to achieve the highest sustainable economic growth and employment and a rising standard of living in Member countries, while maintaining financial stability, and thus to contribute to the development of the world economy;
- to contribute to sound economic expansion in Member as well as non-member countries in the process of economic development; and
- to contribute to the expansion of world trade on a multilateral, non-discriminatory basis in accordance with international obligations.

The original Member countries of the OECD are Austria, Belgium, Canada, Denmark, France, Germany, Greece, Iceland, Ireland, Italy, Luxembourg, the Netherlands, Norway, Portugal, Spain, Sweden, Switzerland, Turkey, the United Kingdom and the United States. The following countries became Members subsequently through accession at the dates indicated hereafter: Japan (28th April 1964), Finland (28th January 1969), Australia (7th June 1971), New Zealand (29th May 1973), Mexico (18th May 1994), the Czech Republic (21st December 1995), Hungary (7th May 1996), Poland (22nd November 1996) and the Republic of Korea (12th December 1996). The Commission of the European Communities takes part in the work of the OECD (Article 13 of the OECD Convention).

Publié en français sous le titre :

PRINCIPAUX INDICATEURS ÉCONOMIQUES
Sources et méthodes
TAUX D'INTÉRÊT ET COURS DES ACTIONS

© OECD 1997
Permission to reproduce a portion of this work for non-commercial purposes or classroom use should be obtained through the Centre français d'exploitation du droit de copie (CFC), 20, rue des Grands-Augustins, 75006 Paris, France, Tel. (33-1) 44 07 47 70, Fax (33-1) 46 34 67 19, for every country except the United States. In the United States permission should be obtained through the Copyright Clearance Center, Customer Service, (508)750-8400, 222 Rosewood Drive, Danvers, MA 01923 USA, or CCC Online: http://www.copyright.com/. All other applications for permission to reproduce or translate all or part of this book should be made to OECD Publications, 2, rue André-Pascal, 75775 Paris Cedex 16, France.

ECONOMIC STATISTICS

For further information on OECD statistical publications, please return the following form to the OECD Publications or visit the OECD web site:

http://www.oecd.org

	Books *Annual Subscription*	***Book*** *Single Issue*	***Diskettes*** *Annual Subscription*	***CD Rom***	***Magnetic tape***
MONTHLY PUBLICATIONS					
Main Economic Indicators	❑ *FF 1 450*	❑ *FF 150*	❑ *FF 6 650*	❑ *FF 25 350*	
Leading Indicators and Business Surveys			❑ *FF 4 750*		
Monthly Statistics of Foreign Trade: Series A	❑ *FF 950*	❑ *FF 110*	❑ *FF 5 100*		❑ *FF 25 250*
QUARTERLY PUBLICATIONS					
Quarterly National Accounts	❑ *FF 450*	❑ *FF 130*	❑ *FF 2 850*		❑ *FF 8 650*
Quarterly Labour Force Statistics	❑ *FF 270*	❑ *FF 90*	❑ *FF 1 700*		❑ *FF 8 650*
Short-Term Economic Indicators: Transition Economies	❑ *FF 350*	❑ *FF 100*	❑ *FF 2 375*		
ANNUAL PUBLICATIONS					
National Accounts					
Volume I: Main aggregates		❑ *FF 220*	❑ *FF 930*		
Volume II: Detailed Tables		❑ *FF 670*	❑ *FF 2 755*		❑ *FF 5 600**
Labour Force Statistics		❑ *FF 550*			❑ *FF 3 500*
International Trade By Commodities Statistics					
SITC Rev. 3	❑ *FF 2 600***	❑ *FF 600*		❑ *FF 2 600*	
Harmonised System				❑ *FF 3 600*	
Services: Statistics on International Transactions		❑ *FF 360*	❑ *FF 930*		
Services: Statistics on Value Added and Employment		❑ *FF 390*	❑ *FF 930*		
Purchasing Power Parities					
Volume I: EKS Results 1993		❑ *FF 145*	❑ *FF 475*		
Volume II: GK Results 1993		❑ *FF 155*	❑ *FF 475*		
International Sectoral Data Base			❑ *FF 3 600*		
Flows and Stocks of Fixed Capital		❑ *FF 140*	❑ *FF 760*		❑ *FF 2 700*
Historical Statistics		❑ *FF 200*	❑ *FF 930*		

(*) Volume I and II *(**) 5 Volumes*

Subscriptions will take effect from the latest issue available, unless instructions to the contrary are received.

❑ Please send me the catalogue of OECD Electronic Publications

❑ I wish to order the above mentioned publications (please mark the publications you wish to order)

❑ Payment is enclosed: Cheque/Money Order

Or charge my card ❑ VISA ❑ MASTERCARD/EUROCARD ❑ AMERICAN EXPRESS

(For orders sent to Paris, you will be charged in French Francs)

Card No.: ______________________

Expiry Date: ______________________

Signature:

Send to*: (Please print)*

Name: ______________________

Address: ______________________

____

Country: ______________________

Fax: ____________ *Tel:* ____________

Please fill out this form legibly and return the entire page by mail or fax to the OECD Publications in Paris (address below), one of the OECD Centres in Bonn, Mexico City, Tokyo or Washington, or to the OECD Distributor in your country (see list at the end of this book).

OECD Publications

2, rue André-Pascal, 75 775 Paris Cedex 16, France

Fax: 33 (0) 1 49 10 42 76 - E-mail: Sales@oecd.org

Sept. 97

STATISTIQUES ÉCONOMIQUES

Pour obtenir des renseignements complémentaires sur les publications statistiques de l'OCDE, retournez ce formulaire aux Éditions de l'OCDE à Paris ou consultez le site internet de l'OCDE :

http://www.oecd.org

	Livres *Abonnement Annuel*	***Livre*** *Au numéro*	***Disquettes*** *Abonnement Annuel*	***CD Rom***	***Bandes Magnétiques***
PUBLICATIONS MENSUELLES					
Principaux indicateurs économiques	❑ *FF 1 450*	❑ *FF 150*	❑ *FF 6 650*	❑ *FF 25 350*	
Indicateurs avancés et enquêtes de conjoncture			❑ *FF 4 750*		
Statistiques mensuelles du commerce extérieur	❑ *FF 950*	❑ *FF 110*	❑ *FF 5 100*		❑ *FF 25 250*
PUBLICATIONS TRIMESTRIELLES					
Comptes nationaux trimestriels	❑ *FF 450*	❑ *FF 130*	❑ *FF 2 850*		❑ *FF 8 650*
Statistiques trimestrielles de la population active	❑ *FF 270*	❑ *FF 90*	❑ *FF 1 700*		❑ *FF 8 650*
Indicateurs économiques à court terme : Économies en transition	❑ *FF 350*	❑ *FF 100*	❑ *FF 2 375*		
PUBLICATIONS ANNUELLES					
Comptes nationaux					
Volume I : Principaux agrégats		❑ *FF 220*	❑ *FF 930*		
Volume II : Tableaux détaillés		❑ *FF 670*	❑ *FF 2 755*		❑ *FF 5 600**
Statistiques de la population active		❑ *FF 550*			❑ *FF 3 500*
Statistiques sur le commerce international par produits					
CTCI Rev. 3	❑ *FF 2 600***	❑ *FF 600*		❑ *FF 2 600*	
Système Harmonisé				❑ *FF 3 600*	
Services: Statistiques sur les échanges internationaux		❑ *FF 360*	❑ *FF 930*		
Services: Statistiques sur la valeur ajoutée et l'emploi		❑ *FF 390*	❑ *FF 930*		
Parités de Pouvoir d'Achat					
Volume I : Résultats EKS 1993		❑ *FF 145*	❑ *FF 475*		
Volume II : Résultats GK 1993		❑ *FF 155*	❑ *FF 475*		
Base de données sectorielles internationales (ISDB)			❑ *FF 3 600*		
Flux et stocks de capital fixe		❑ *FF 140*	❑ *FF 760*		❑ *FF 2 700*
Statistiques rétrospectives		❑ *FF 200*	❑ *FF 930*		

(*) Volume I et II (**) 5 Volumes

Sauf indication contraire, les abonnements prendront effet à partir du dernier numéro paru.

❑ Veuillez m'envoyer le catalogue des éditions électroniques

❑ Je souhaite commander les publications mentionnées ci-dessus (veuillez cocher les cases correspondantes)

❑ Règlement joint : Chèque/Mandat

Ou débitez ma carte ❑ VISA ❑ MASTERCARD/EUROCARD ❑ AMERICAN EXPRESS

(Pour les commandes envoyées à Paris, vous serez facturé en francs français)

N° de carte: ______________________

Date d'expiration: ______________________

Signature:

***Adresse d'expédition**: (Ecrire en majuscules)*

Nom : ______________________

Adresse : ______________________

____

Pays : ______________________

Fax : ____________ *Tél. :* ____________

Veuillez remplir ce formulaire et le retourner par courier ou fax aux Éditions de l'OCDE à Paris (adresse ci-dessous), à l'un des Centres de l'OCDE à Bonn, Mexico, Tokyo, ou Washington, ou au distributeur de l'OCDE dans votre pays (c.f. liste à la fin de cet ouvrage).

Les Éditions de l'OCDE

2, rue André-Pascal, 75 775 Paris Cedex 16, France

Fax: 33 (0) 1 49 10 42 76 - Internet: Sales@oecd.org

sept. 97

MAIN ECONOMIC INDICATORS

This publication is the essential source of short-term statistics for OECD Member countries. It provides a complete and timely picture of the most recent changes in the economies of the OECD countries and puts them in an international context. The indicators selected cover:

- National Accounts
- Business Surveys
- Deliveries, Stocks and Orders
- Domestic Trade
- Wages
- Foreign Finance
- Foreign Trade
- Industrial Production
- Money and Domestic Finance
- Construction
- Labour
- Prices
- Interest Rates
- Balance of Payments

The corresponding monthly diskette gives ten years of monthly or quarterly time series for the same indicators, documented electronically and easy to select for your own analysis. *Now also available on CD-ROM!*

SHORT - TERM ECONOMIC INDICATORS: TRANSITION ECONOMIES

Similar to the *Main Economic Indicators* in choice and presentation of statistics, the *Short Term Economic Indicators* presents data for those transition economies in Central and Eastern Europe and the New Independent States (NIS) that are adapting their statistics to meet international standards and the needs of market economies. It thus constitutes an invaluable source of information for analysing short-term economic developments in individual transition economies, and for undertaking comparative analysis of these developments. In all, 20 countries are included in this quarterly publication, presenting an enlightening picture of a rapidly changing economic area.

An annual subscription on diskette also covers the supply of historical figures from 1980. Both editions include an annual printed methodological supplement.

QUARTERLY NATIONAL ACCOUNTS

This publication contains a selection of the accounts which are the most used for economic analysis. GDP by type of expenditure and by kind of activity, gross fixed capital formation by sectors and by type of goods and private final consumption by type of expenditure and by object are shown at both current and constant prices. Financing of capital formation and GDP by cost structure are shown at current prices.

The data cover 21 Member countries and the following groups of countries: OECD, NAFTA, OECD-Europe, European Union and the Major 7 (G-7).

The printed publication gives annual and quarterly data for the last 15 years. The electronic publication and the tape give, whenever possible, data back to 1970 and 1950 respectively.

LEADING INDICATORS AND BUSINESS SURVEYS

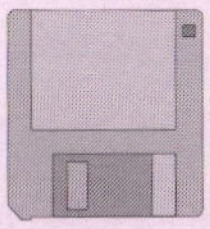

This monthly diskette contains the extensive information from Business Surveys in OECD countries, in which business managers describe their perception of current and future developments of important business indicators. It also contains composite leading indicators and their components, giving the essential information needed for detecting early signals on turning points in business cycles. The diskette contains ten to twenty years of monthly or quarterly time series, easy to select for your own analysis.

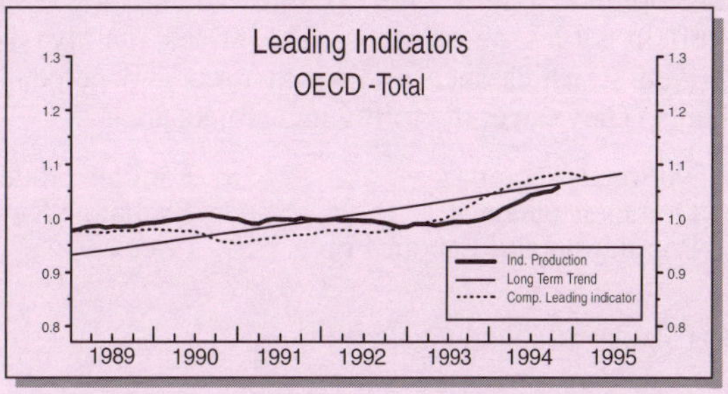

In total, some 1 000 series are updated monthly. These prompt cyclical data are a valuable aid to economic analysis and forecasting.

NATIONAL ACCOUNTS: Volume I – Main Aggregates

Included are tables showing the main aggregates of the national accounts, from final expenditures on the GDP to net saving and current surplus; growth triangles; purchasing power parities; comparative tables of real growth and inflation; data for each Member country and for all OECD, OECD-Europe and the European Union.

The printed publication covers the last 30 years. The diskette and magnetic tape cover the period from 1960 so far as data are available.

OCDE — TOTAL

Principaux Agrégats basés sur les taux de change

milliards de dollars É-U

1981	1982	1983	1984	1985	1986	1987	1988	1989	1990	1991	1992	1993	1994	1995	
															DÉPENSES IMPUTÉES AU P.I.B.
															Aux prix courants et taux de change de 1990
1475.48	1611.42	1733.79	1857.15	1997.27	2133.12	2264.99	2405.74	2548.80	2769.20	2978.95	3163.00	3314.07	3478.90	3738.14	1. Consommation finale des administrations publiques
5253.25	5690.50	6166.82	6662.05	7187.63	7666.28	8214.73	8890.69	9610.22	10368.47	11057.32	11814.64	12561.76	13672.54	15349.56	2. Consommation finale privée
..	..	..	..	..	..	..	..	..	..	..	..	..	..	..	3. Ménages

IRELAND **IRLANDE**

Average per cent changes at annual rate

	1983	1984	1985	1986	1987	1988	1989	1990	1991	1992	1993	1994	1995
1982	-1.0	1.3	1.8	1.2	1.9	2.3	3.1	3.8	3.6	3.6	3.6	3.9	4.3
1983		3.6	3.2	2.0	2.6	3.0	3.8	4.5	4.1	4.1	4.0	4.3	4.8
1984			2.8	1.1	2.3	2.8	3.8	4.6	4.2	4.2	4.1	4.4	4.9
1985				-0.5	2.1	2.9	4.0	5.0	4.5	4.4	4.2	4.5	5.1
1986					4.6	4.6	5.6	6.4	5.5	5.2	4.9	5.2	5.8
1987						4.5	6.1	6.9	5.7	5.3	5.0	5.3	5.9
1988	**G.D.P. per head**						7.7	8.2	6.1	5.5	5.1	5.4	6.1
1989	(volume)							8.7	5.3	4.8	4.4	5.0	5.8
1990	**P.I.B. par tête**								2.0	2.9	3.0	4.0	5.3
1991	(volume)									3.9	3.6	4.7	6.1
1992											3.2	5.2	6.9
1993												7.1	8.7
1994													10.4

Variations moyennes en pourcentage aux taux annuels

	1983	1984	1985	1986	1987	1988	1989	1990	1991	1992	1993	1994	1995
1982	0.1	0.7	1.9	1.9	2.2	2.6	3.4	3.3	3.1	3.2	3.0	3.3	3.3
1983		1.3	2.8	2.5	2.7	3.1	3.9	3.7	3.5	3.5	3.3	3.6	3.6
1984			4.3	3.1	3.2	3.5	4.5	4.1	3.8	3.8	3.5	3.8	3.8
1985				2.0	2.6	3.3	4.5	4.1	3.7	3.7	3.4	3.8	3.7
1986					3.3	3.9	5.4	4.7	4.1	4.0	3.6	4.0	3.9
1987						4.6	6.5	5.1	4.3	4.1	3.7	4.1	4.0
1988							8.4	5.4	4.2	4.0	3.5	4.0	3.9
1989	**Private final consumption expenditure per head**							2.5	2.1	2.6	2.3	3.1	3.2
1990	(volume)								1.7	2.7	2.2	3.3	3.3
1991	**Consommation finale privée par tête**									3.7	2.5	3.8	3.7
1992	(volume)										1.3	3.9	3.7
1993												6.6	5.0
1994													3.4

NATIONAL ACCOUNTS: Volume II – Detailed Tables

Twenty-one standard tables give detailed statistics, so far as data are available, for Member countries:

- Main aggregates of National Accounts
- Consumption expenditure at current and constant prices
- Gross fixed capital formation at current and constant prices
- Costs components of value added by kind of activity
- Employment by kind of activity
- Income and outlay, and capital accounts by institutional sectors.

The printed publication covers 13 years. The diskettes and magnetic tapes go back for longer periods depending on data availability.

FOREIGN TRADE BY COMMODITIES

Also referred to as "Series C", the main foreign trade data base of the OECD gives the imports and exports of its Member countries in values (thousands of US dollar) and in quantities, broken down by type of commodity and by partner country. Data are classified according to the SITC (Standard International Trade Classification) or HS (Harmonised System) and are available from 1961 for most Member countries.

The printed publication - Foreign Trade by Commodities - is in five volumes and gives values of trade by broad commodity sections and divisions and by partner country for the last six years.

NEW! The CD-ROM version, ITCS: International Trade by Commodity Statistics, gives full commodity and partner country detail in values and quantities from 1961 as far as data are available.

HISTORICAL STATISTICS

This publication provides an overview of the economic development of the Member countries of the OECD since 1960 in tables and graphs. The tables mainly show derived statistics such as growth rates and percentage shares. They cover the following subject areas:

- National Accounts
- Domestic Finance
- Population and Labour Force
- Foreign Trade
- Exchange Rates
- Prices

It is also available on diskette.

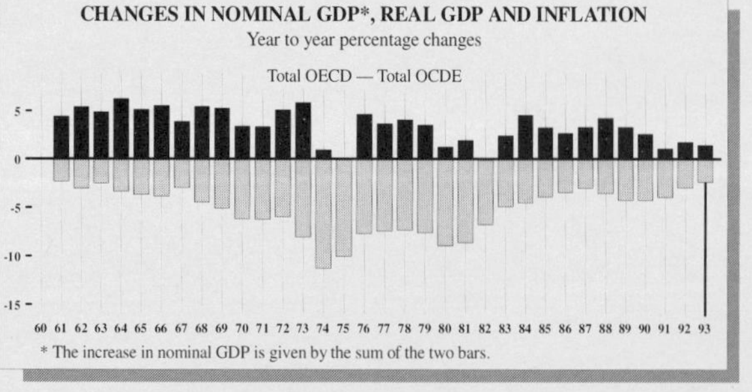

LABOUR FORCE STATISTICS

Detailed statistics on population, labour force, employment and unemployment, broken down by sex, employment status and kind of activity. This publication also provides participation and unemployment rates by sex and detailed age groups and comparative tables for the main components of the labour force. Data are available for each OECD Member country and for all OECD, OECD-Europe and the European Union.

The printed publication covers 21 years for the main tables. The magnetic tapes cover the period from 1960 so far as data are available.

QUARTERLY LABOUR FORCE STATISTICS

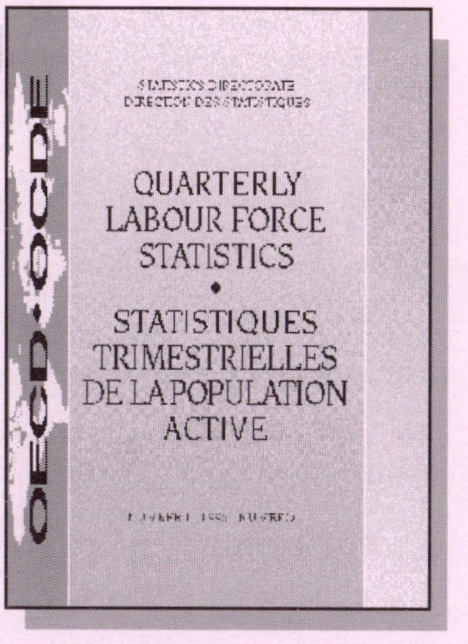

Included are tables showing total and civilian labour force, unemployment by age and sex, broad industry breakdown of employment, unemployment rates and youth unemployment. This publication also provides standardised unemployment rates to permit comparisons for 17 OECD countries.

The printed publication contains data for the last 23 quarters. The diskette version contains quarterly data from 1961 so far as data are available.

PURCHASING POWER PARITIES AND REAL EXPENDITURES

Data are presented on Purchasing Power Parities (PPPs) for all OECD Member Countries for GDP as a whole and for over 50 expenditure categories for benchmark years. Analytical tables compare PPPs, price levels and real expenditures between countries.

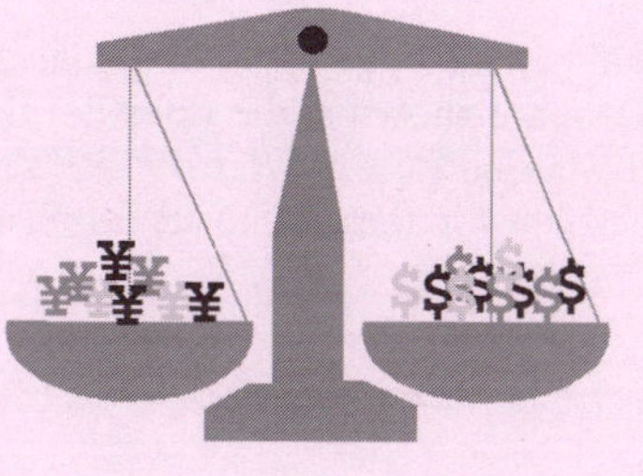

The printed and diskette versions of this publication are identical. The latest issue refers to 1993.

The next benchmark year will be 1996, for which results will be published early in 1998.

INTERNATIONAL SECTORAL DATABASE (ISDB)

Standardised data are provided for 30 industry groups in 14 OECD Member countries on:

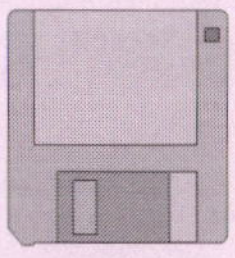

- Value Added in current and constant prices
- Compensation of Employees
- Total Employment
- Capital Stock
- Foreign Trade
- Net Indirect Taxes
- Gross Operating Surplus
- Number of Employees
- Investment
- Total Factor Productivity Index

Series are broken down according to the International Standard Industrial Classification (ISIC revision 2). So far as data are available, series cover the period from 1960 to 1995. The ISDB is a corporate data bank which has been specially designed to optimise data availability and comparability. It regroups comparable data drawn from several sources under the same simple computer system. It allows instantaneous labour and capital productivity calculation at a detailed sectoral level. The 1996 issue includes number of hours actually worked and capital consumption data.

MONTHLY STATISTICS OF FOREIGN TRADE: Series A

The core of this publication shows the trade of individual OECD Member countries and main country groupings with most of their partner countries. In addition, tables show the trade of the main country groupings of the OECD (adjusted and unadjusted for seasonal variations), the trade by SITC section (original figures) and volume and average value indices.

Longer historical series and more detailed data are available on tape. Trade by SITC section by volume and average value indices are available on diskette.

FLOWS AND STOCKS OF FIXED CAPITAL

This publication contains information on gross stock, net stock, gross fixed capital formation and capital consumption at constant and current prices for all OECD countries for which these data are available. It thus constitutes an essential source of information for undertaking productivity analysis. A more detailed breakdown by industry is available on magnetic tape or in the International Sectoral Data Base (ISDB) diskette.

SERVICES: STATISTICS ON INTERNATIONAL TRANSACTIONS

Data presented show the overall trends in international trade in services, synoptic tables for the 20 most important types of services and country tables showing the maximum detail available on international transactions in service activities.

The printed publication and the diskette both cover the period from 1970 so far as data are available.

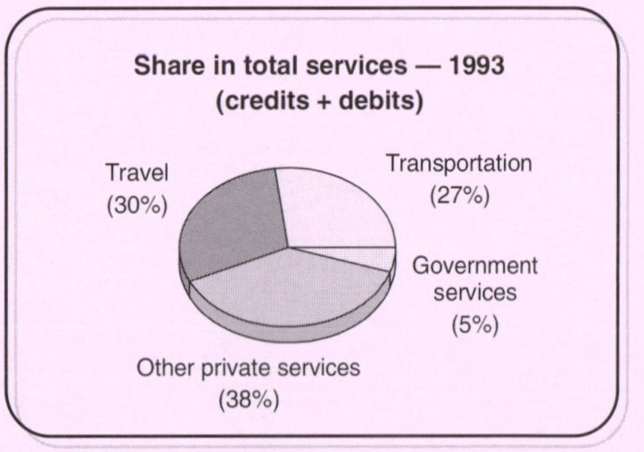

SERVICES: STATISTICS ON VALUE ADDED AND EMPLOYMENT

Value added at current and constant prices and employment in service activities in 26 OECD Member countries. Data are shown at the finest level of detail available in national sources. So far as data are available, series cover the period from 1970 to 1995. The data base is designed for analysis of levels and growth of productivity in service activities in the OECD area. It is available in printed form and on diskette.

FOREIGN TRADE EXTRACTION — TAILOR MADE

Customers can order their own special extraction from annual and monthly OECD Foreign Trade data bases as listings or copied to diskettes or tape. Imports and exports by commodity according to the UN Standard International Trade Classification (SITC) and by partner country are available in thousands of US dollars and in quantities from 1961 to present.

For further information and details of charges, please contact Foreign Trade extraction service:

Telefax: (33 1) 45 24 96 57 **Internet:** *stat.contact@oecd.org*

PRINCIPAUX INDICATEURS ÉCONOMIQUES

Cette publication est une source indispensable pour les statistiques de court terme des pays Membres de l'OCDE. Elle fournit une image complète et à jour des changements les plus récents intervenus dans les économies des pays Membres de l'OCDE et les situe dans un contexte international. Les indicateurs sélectionnés couvrent :

- Comptes nationaux
- Enquêtes de conjoncture
- Livraisons, stocks et commandes
- Commerce intérieur
- Salaires
- Finances extérieures
- Commerce extérieur
- Production industrielle
- Masse monétaire et finances internes
- Construction
- Emploi
- Prix
- Taux d'intérêt
- Balance des paiements

Les disquettes correspondantes contiennent dix ans de données mensuelles ou trimestrielles pour ces indicateurs, documentées électroniquement et faciles à sélectionner pour votre propre analyse. *Maintenant disponible en CD-ROM aussi!*

INDICATEURS ÉCONOMIQUES A COURT TERME : ÉCONOMIES EN TRANSITION

Semblables aux *Principaux Indicateurs Économiques* quant au choix des statistiques et à la présentation, les *Indicateurs Économiques à court terme* présentent les données se rapportant aux pays en transition d'Europe centrale et orientale et aux Nouveaux États Indépendants (NEI) qui mettent en conformité leurs statistiques avec les normes internationales et les adaptent aux impératifs d'une économie de marché. Elle constitue donc une source d'information irremplaçable pour analyser les évolutions économiques à court terme dans chaque économie en transition et pour entreprendre des analyses comparatives. En tout, 20 pays sont inclus dans cette publication trimestrielle, présentant un éclairage sur les transformations rapides de cette zone économique.

Une souscription annuelle aux disquettes permet d'obtenir également les données historiques à partir de 1980. Les deux éditions incluent un supplément méthodologique annuel (imprimé).

COMPTES NATIONAUX TRIMESTRIELS

Cette publication contient une sélection des comptes les plus utilisés pour l'analyse économique. Le PIB par emploi et par genre d'activité, la formation brute de capital fixe par secteurs et par type de biens et la consommation finale privée par catégorie et par fonction sont publiés aux prix courants et constants. Le PIB par répartition et le financement de la formation de capital sont présentés aux prix courants.

Les données concernent 21 pays Membres ainsi que les groupes de pays suivants : OCDE, ALENA, OCDE-Europe, Union européenne et les Sept grands pays (G7).

L'ouvrage imprimé contient des données annuelles et trimestrielles pour les 15 dernières années. La disquette et la bande magnétique fournissent des données respectivement à partir de 1970 et de 1950 dans tous les cas où c'est possible.

INDICATEURS AVANCÉS ET ENQUÊTES DE CONJONCTURE

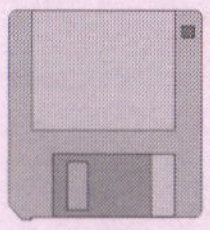

Cette disquette mensuelle contient un volume très important d'informations provenant des enquêtes de conjoncture menées dans les pays de l'OCDE, dans lesquelles les dirigeants d'entreprises donnent leur perception des mouvements courants et anticipés d'une sélection d'indicateurs économiques prépondérants. La disquette contient aussi des indicateurs composites avancés ainsi que leurs composantes, donnant ainsi l'information essentielle pour la détection des points de retournement du cycle économique.

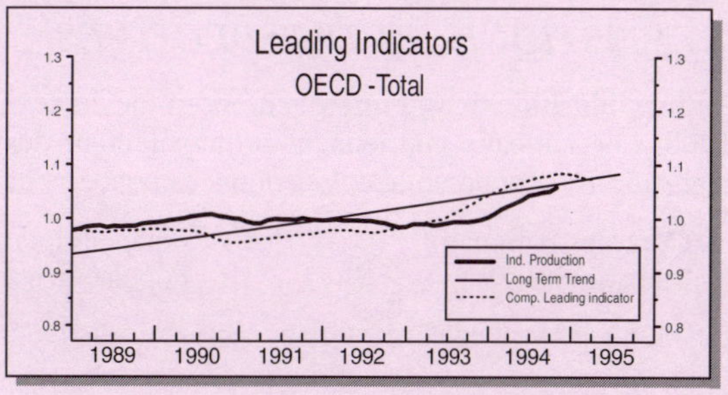

Les disquettes contiennent dix ans de données mensuelles ou trimestrielles pour ces indicateurs, faciles à sélectionner pour votre propre analyse.

COMPTES NATIONAUX : Volume 1 – Principaux agrégats

Cette publication présente les principaux agrégats des comptes nationaux, allant des emplois finals du PIB à l'épargne nette et à l'excédent de balance courante ; triangles de croissance ; parités de pouvoir d'achat ; tableaux comparatifs de la croissance réelle et de l'inflation ; données relatives à chaque pays Membre, ainsi qu'à l'ensemble de la zone OCDE, aux pays européens de l'OCDE et à l'Union européenne.

L'ouvrage imprimé couvre les 30 dernières années. La disquette et la bande magnétique couvrent la période écoulée depuis 1960, en fonction de la disponibilité des données.

OCDE — TOTAL

Principaux Agrégats basés sur les taux de change

milliards de dollars É-U

1981	1982	1983	1984	1985	1986	1987	1988	1989	1990	1991	1992	1993	1994	1995	DÉPENSES IMPUTÉES AU P.I.B. *Aux prix courants et taux de change de 1990*
1475.48	1611.42	1733.79	1857.15	1997.27	2133.12	2264.99	2405.74	2548.80	2769.20	2978.95	3163.00	3314.07	3478.90	3738.14	1. Consommation finale des administrations publiques
5253.25	5690.50	6166.82	6662.05	7187.63	7666.28	8214.73	8890.69	9610.22	10368.47	11057.32	11814.64	12561.76	13672.54	15349.56	2. Consommation finale privée
															3. Ménages

IRELAND — **IRLANDE**

Average per cent changes at annual rate

G.D.P. per head (volume)
P.I.B. par tête (volume)

	1983	1984	1985	1986	1987	1988	1989	1990	1991	1992	1993	1994	1995
1982	-1.0	1.3	1.8	1.2	1.9	2.3	3.1	3.8	3.6	3.6	3.6	3.9	4.3
1983		3.6	3.2	2.0	2.6	3.0	3.8	4.5	4.1	4.1	4.0	4.3	4.8
1984			2.8	1.1	2.3	2.8	3.8	4.6	4.2	4.2	4.1	4.4	4.9
1985				-0.5	2.1	2.9	4.0	5.0	4.5	4.4	4.2	4.5	5.1
1986					4.6	4.6	5.6	6.4	5.5	5.2	4.9	5.2	5.8
1987						4.5	6.1	6.9	5.7	5.3	5.0	5.3	5.9
1988							7.7	8.2	6.1	5.5	5.1	5.4	6.1
1989								8.7	5.3	4.8	4.4	5.0	5.8
1990									2.0	2.9	3.0	4.0	5.3
1991										3.9	3.6	4.7	6.1
1992											3.2	5.2	6.9
1993												7.1	8.7
1994													10.4

Variations moyennes en pourcentage aux taux annuels

Private final consumption expenditure per head (volume)
Consommation finale privée par tête (volume)

	1983	1984	1985	1986	1987	1988	1989	1990	1991	1992	1993	1994	1995
1982	0.1	0.7	1.9	1.9	2.2	2.6	3.4	3.3	3.1	3.2	3.0	3.3	3.3
1983		1.3	2.8	2.5	2.7	3.1	3.9	3.7	3.5	3.5	3.3	3.6	3.6
1984			4.3	3.1	3.2	3.5	4.5	4.1	3.8	3.8	3.5	3.8	3.8
1985				2.0	2.6	3.3	4.5	4.1	3.7	3.7	3.4	3.8	3.7
1986					3.3	3.9	5.4	4.7	4.1	4.0	3.6	4.0	3.9
1987						4.6	6.5	5.1	4.3	4.1	3.7	4.1	4.0
1988							8.4	5.4	4.2	4.0	3.5	4.0	3.9
1989								2.5	2.1	2.6	2.3	3.1	3.2
1990									1.7	2.7	2.2	3.3	3.3
1991										3.7	2.5	3.8	3.7
1992											1.3	3.9	3.7
1993												6.6	5.0
1994													3.4

COMPTES NATIONAUX : Volume II – Tableaux détaillés

Vingt et un tableaux standardisés présentent des statistiques détaillées, pour les Pays Membres, sur les sujets suivants :

- Principaux agrégats des Comptes Nationaux,
- Consommation finale privée, prix courants et prix constants,
- Formation brute de capital fixe, prix courants et constants,
- Coûts constitutifs de la valeur ajoutée par genre d'activité,
- Emploi par genre d'activité,
- Compte de revenu et de dépenses, comptes de capital par secteurs institutionnels.

L'ouvrage imprimé couvre 13 années. Les disquettes et les bandes magnétiques couvrent des périodes plus longues, en fonction de la disponibilité des données.

COMMERCE EXTÉRIEUR PAR PRODUITS

Egalement connue sous le nom de "séries C", la principale base de données de l'OCDE sur le commerce extérieur fournit des données sur les importations et les exportations de ses pays Membres en valeurs (milliers de dollars) et en quantités, par type de produits et par pays partenaire. Les données sont classées selon la CTCI (Classification du Commerce International) ou selon SH (Système Harmonisé) et sont disponibles à partir de 1961 pour la plupart des pays Membres.

La publication - Commerce extérieur par produits - se présente en 5 volumes et fournit des données par sections et divisions des principaux produits et par pays partenaire pour les 6 dernières années.

NOUVEAU! La version sur CD ROM - ITCS (Statistiques sur le Commerce International par Produit) - fournit l'ensemble du détail par produit et par pays partenaire en valeurs et en quantités à partir de 1961, dans la mesure où les données sont disponibles.

STATISTIQUES RÉTROSPECTIVES

Cette publication fournit une vue d'ensemble du développement économique des pays Membres de l'OCDE depuis 1960. Les tableaux contiennent principalement des statistiques dérivées comme des taux de croissance et des répartitions en pourcentage. Les données concernent des domaines tels que :

- Comptes nationaux
- Finances internes
- Commerce extérieur
- Taux de change
- Population et population active
- Prix

Les données sont également disponibles sur disquette.

STATISTIQUES SUR LA POPULATION ACTIVE

Statistiques détaillées sur la population, la population active, l'emploi et le chômage, décomposées par sexe, situation dans la profession et type d'activité. Cette publication fournit également des taux d'activité et des taux de chômage par sexe et tranche d'âge, ainsi que des tableaux comparatifs portant sur les principales composantes de la population active. Les données sont disponibles pour chaque pays Membre et pour les zones OCDE, pays européens de l'OCDE et Union Européenne.

La publication couvre 21 années pour les principaux tableaux. Les bandes magnétiques couvrent la période qui s'étend de 1960 à l'année la plus récente disponible.

STATISTIQUES TRIMESTRIELLES DE LA POPULATION ACTIVE

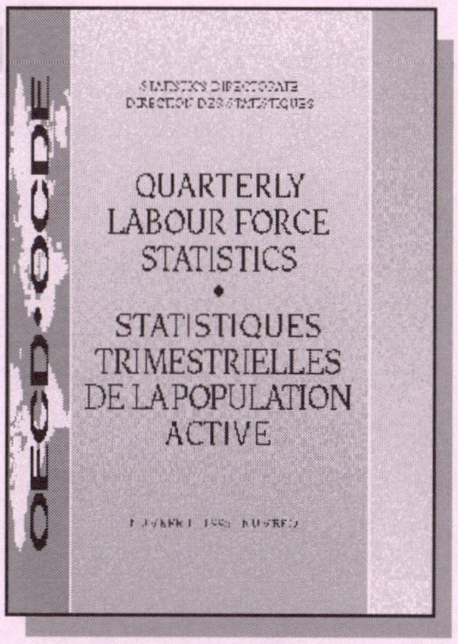

Cette publication fournit des données sur la population active totale et civile, le chômage par âge et sexe, la décomposition par branche d'activité principale de l'emploi, le taux de chômage et le chômage des jeunes. Cette publication fournit également des taux de chômage standardisés permettant des comparaisons entre 17 pays Membres de l'OCDE.

La publication fournit des données pour les 23 derniers trimestres. La version sur disquette fournit des données à partir de 1961 jusqu'à l'année la plus récente disponible.

PARITÉS DE POUVOIR D'ACHAT ET DÉPENSES RÉELLES

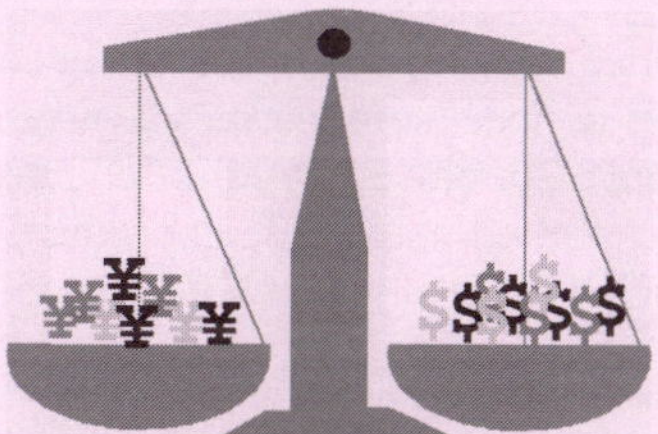

Cette publication fournit des Parités de Pouvoir d'Achat (PPA) pour tous les pays Membres de l'OCDE au niveau du PIB total et de 50 catégories de dépense pour l'année de référence. Des tableaux analytiques comparent les PPA, les niveaux de prix et les dépenses réelles entre les pays.

Les contenus de la publication et des disquettes sont identiques. La dernière édition concerne les données de l'année 1993. La prochaine année de référence sera 1996. Les résultats seront publiés au début de l'année 1998.

BASE DE DONNÉES SECTORIELLES INTERNATIONALES (ISDB)

Cette disquette contient des données standardisées pour trente groupes d'industrie et quatorze pays Membres de l'OCDE sur :

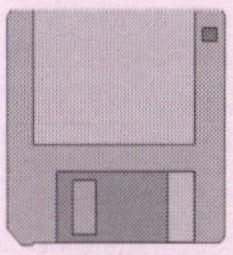

- Valeur ajoutée à prix courant et constant
- Rémunération des salariés
- Emploi total
- Stock de capital,
- Commerce extérieur
- Impôts indirects nets
- Excédent brut d'exploitation
- Nombre de salariés
- Investissement
- Indice de productivité totale des facteurs

Les industries sont définies selon la Classification Internationale Type par Industrie (CITI révision 2). Dans la mesure où les données sont disponibles, les séries couvrent la période de 1960 à 1995. ISDB est une base de données qui a été spécialement conçue pour optimiser la disponibilité et la comparabilité des données. Elle regroupe dans un format informatique simple des données comparables issues de plusieurs sources. ISDB permet des calculs instantanés de la productivité du travail et du capital à un niveau sectoriel. L'édition 1996 inclut le nombre d'heures réellement travaillées et des données sur la consommation de capital.

STATISTIQUES MENSUELLES DU COMMERCE EXTÉRIEUR: Séries A

Cette publication montre pour l'essentiel le commerce de chacun des pays Membres de l'OCDE et des principaux groupes de pays avec la plupart de leurs pays partenaires. Par ailleurs, des tableaux montrent le commerce des grands groupes de pays de l'OCDE (en chiffres bruts et corrigés des variations saisonnières) ainsi que le commerce par section de la CTCI (chiffres bruts) et des indices de volume et de valeur moyenne.

Des séries historiques plus longues et plus détaillées sont disponibles sur bande magnétique. Les données du commerce par section de la CTCI et les indices de volume et de valeur moyenne sont également disponibles sur disquette.

FLUX ET STOCKS DE CAPITAL FIXE

Cette publication présente des données de stock brut, stock net, formation de capital fixe et consommation de capital fixe à prix courants et constants pour tous les pays Membres de l'OCDE pour lesquels ces données sont disponibles. Elle est, de ce fait, une source d'information essentielle pour entreprendre des analyses de productivité. Des données plus détaillées par industrie sont disponibles sur bande magnétique ou dans la disquette de la Base de Données Sectorielles Internationales (ISDB).

SERVICES : STATISTIQUES SUR LES ECHANGES INTERNATIONAUX

Cette publication présente les tendances globales dans les échanges internationaux de services, tableaux synoptiques pour les 20 principaux types de service et tableaux par pays indiquant le maximum de détail disponible sur les échanges internationaux de service.

La publication et les disquettes couvrent toutes les deux la période qui s'étend de 1970 à l'année la plus récente disponible.

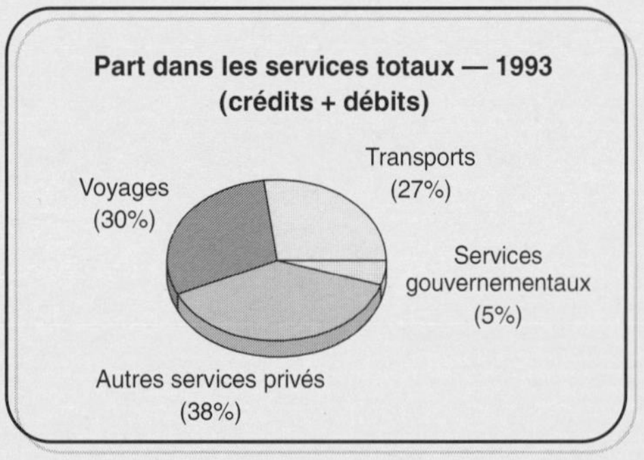

SERVICES: STATISTIQUES SUR LA VALEUR AJOUTÉE ET L'EMPLOI

Valeur ajoutée à prix courant et constant et emploi dans les activités de service pour 26 pays Membres de l'OCDE. Les données sont fournies au niveau le plus fin disponible dans les sources nationales. Dans la mesure où les données sont disponibles, les séries couvrent la période qui s'étend de 1970 à 1995. Cette base de donnée a été conçue pour permettre l'analyse de la productivité en termes de niveaux et de croissance dans les activités de service de la zone OCDE. Les données sont disponibles sous forme de publication et de disquettes.

EXTRACTIONS DES DONNÉES DU COMMERCE EXTÉRIEUR

Les clients peuvent commander des extractions spécifiques sur disquettes, bande magnétique ou papier de la base de données annuelle ou mensuelle du Commerce Extérieur de l'OCDE. Les importations et les exportations par produits selon la Classification Type du Commerce International des Nations Unies (CTCI) et par pays partenaire sont disponibles en milliers de dollars américains, et en quantité depuis 1961.

Pour plus de renseignements ou de détails sur les conditions de paiement, veuillez contacter le service d'extraction du Commerce Extérieur :

Telefax: (33 1) 45 24 96 57 **Internet:** *stat.contact@oecd.org*

Table of contents

Supplements to Main Economic Indicators

HISTORICAL STATISTICS

Historical data and sources and definitions for all series published in Main Economic Indicators are also available on MEI on Statwise diskettes and on CD-ROM. Sets of diskettes cover the latest 10-year period and each of the decades 1960-1969, 1970-1979 and 1980-1989. The CD-ROM includes data from 1960, where available.

SOURCES AND METHODS

This supplement is published in occasional instalments dealing either with one country's statistics on all subjects or with statistics for all countries on a particular subject. Each booklet refers in principle to the selection of series contained in the issue of Main Economic Indicators with which it was released. Those published since 1980 are listed below:

By subject:

Business Surveys: No. 37, April 1983.

OECD Leading Indicators and Business Cycles in Member countries: No. 39, January 1987.

Consumer Price Indices: Special issue, April 1994.

Producer Price Indices: Special issue, April 1994.

Labour and Wage Statistics: Sources and Methods, April 1997.

Domestic Finance: Sources and Methods, October 1997 (forthcoming).

By country:

Mexico: Sources and Methods, December 1996.

Korea: Sources and Methods, March 1997.

SOURCES AND DEFINITIONS

Sources and definitions of the statistics included in Part One and Part Two are available in English on the Internet (http://www.oecd.org/std/mei.htm):

The latest printed edition is as follows:

Main Economic Indicators - Sources and Definitions 1997, July 1997

1. Introduction

The monthly 'Main Economic Indicators' (MEI) publication includes statistics on interest rates and share prices. Definitions of the various interest series published and details on the methodologies used by Member countries in their compilation of the share price indices shown are presented herein and reflect series as published in the December 1997 issue of the MEI.

A. INTEREST RATES

To define interest is a relatively simple matter. Interest can be said to be the price paid by the borrower for the use of funds saved by the lender and the compensation to the lender for his deferring expenditures. This compensation comprises two elements, namely a payment equal to the loss of purchasing power of the principal during the term of the loan and a balance that represents the real interest accruing to the lender.

However this simplicity does not extend into the area of rate determination since rates vary not only because of inflation, as implied above, but also because of a number of other influences, including:

- The amount, purpose and period of the transaction;
- The credit-worthiness of the borrower;
- The collateral offered and/or other guarantees/guarantors available;
- The competition for the transaction;
- Government policy.

As a consequence, there will be numerous rates applying to the large number of transactions that are in effect at any one time in any one country. For the rates shown in the Main Economic Indicators publication, where the intent is to present those most suitable for use in economic analysis, the task is thus one of selection. Ideally, for each Member country, the interest rates chosen should include those which are used as a reference for the determination of other rates, whether fixed (by the authorities or by agreements between financial institutions) or resulting from the interaction of supply and demand. They should also include those that are representative of the most important borrowing or investment instruments.

While efforts have been made in the rate selection to ensure as much international comparability as possible, the fact remains that the institutional features of each member's financial markets are distinct and often markedly different from those of other members. However, the intent is to present for each country a range of rates, from 'overnight' through 'short-term' to 'long-term'. In general, 'overnight' and 'short term' rates relate to money market instruments, while 'long term' rates are secondary market yields of long term (usually 10 year) bonds.

Overnight is here used as a term to describe official discount rates and call-money rates. The official discount rate is the rate at which central banks make advances to, or discount eligible bills of exchange for, selected banks and other financial intermediaries. There are often strict rules regarding the quality of securities which will be accepted as collateral for the advances and regarding the eligibility of bills of exchange to be discounted. In the case of the latter, normally they must be of limited duration to maturity, commercial and not financial paper, and guaranteed by parties known to be solvent. Additionally, there are limits on the amount of credit available.

Call money and day-to-day loans play a predominant role in interbank money dealings and between banks and money market dealers. Day-to-day loans usually refer to operations on the money market between banks to balance temporary surpluses and shortages of liquidity. These operations are sometimes conducted through the central bank. Call money generally refers to secured or unsecured 'at-call' loans made by banks to money market dealers. It is occasionally used for the flow of funds from financial institutions with an excess of their own funds and deposits (in relation to customers' demands) to institutions with a shortage.

Short term rates are usually either the three month interbank offer rate attaching to loans given and taken amongst banks for any excess or shortage of liquidity over several months or the rate associated with Treasury bills, Certificates of Deposit or comparable instruments, each of three month maturity.

Long term (in most cases 10 year) government bonds are the instrument whose yield is used as the representative 'interest rate' for this area. Generally the yield is calculated at the pre-tax level and before deductions for brokerage costs and commissions and is derived from the relationship between the present market value of the bond and that at maturity, taking into account also interest payments paid through to maturity.

Monthly figures shown are calculated as the average of weighted or unweighted arithmetic rates relating to all days or specified days in the month or they refer to a day at or near month's end. For short and long term interest rates, annual and quarterly data are normally averages of monthly figures, while for 'overnight' rates, annual and quarterly data usually refer to the figure for the final month of the period.

In nearly all instances, data are provided by the central bank, the exception being the Monetary Institute of Luxembourg.

B. SHARE PRICE INDICES

General

This report is intended as a summary of the sources and methods employed by the source agencies, primarily the stock exchanges of the Member countries, in their compilation of share price indices. It seems appropriate, however, to comment first on the choice of the indices published.

Index Selection

Given that in most countries there is more than one index, occasionally more than one stock exchange, an initial task was to determine the choice of the index to be included. The aim was to secure that index which would best suit the need for economic analysis. A consultative process involving OECD Member countries, Eurostat, the Commission of European Communities and OECD's Directorate for Financial, Fiscal and Enterprise Affairs resulted in the establishment of a set of selection criteria. It was fully accepted that not all elements would necessarily be attained in all countries, but the expectation was that, for the index chosen, the more important criteria would be met.

In concise form the criteria comprised the following:

(a) Since the index needed is the one best suited for economic analysis and thus an index measuring market performance, it should be a price index and not a return index. A return index is one relating to the return realised by an investor and is constructed on the basis that dividends and similar payments are assumed to be re-invested. In contrast, a price index excludes re-invested monies and reflects only changes in share prices themselves.

(b) The index should cover all stock exchanges in a country or, failing this, the principal exchange.

(c) To eliminate double counting, the index should exclude units of investment funds. Additionally, foreign companies, comprising both non-resident companies and resident companies whose head offices are located abroad, should be excluded. However, there is always likely to be an element of double counting since major companies have pension funds which own shares in other companies.

(d) The index should track all share prices or, failing this, those of shares most heavily traded or those of companies with the greatest market capitalization.

(e) Weighting should relate to market capitalization and not to factors such as share prices, trading volume, etc.

(f) The index should be calculated as the average of daily indices over the month.

Indices for 27 of the 29 Member countries are published in the monthly Main Economic Indicators, with only Hungary and Luxembourg not presently included. Descriptions are given for each of these 27 countries.

Although primarily designed as measurements of market performance for use by individual investors and investment fund managers, share price indices are also used as indicators of economic activity by business and government analysts. It is for this reason that they are included in a publication entitled 'Main Economic Indicators'. They are presented as stand alone measures but they also have a crucial role as a component in the construction of the 'composite leading indicators' series. Leading indicators are aggregate time series displaying a reasonably consistent advance relationship with a reference series measuring the economic cycle of a country, usually the index of industrial production. The OECD presently publishes composite leading indicators for 22 Member countries. As a gauge of the effectiveness of share price indices as reliable pointers to future economic activity, it is interesting to note that they are a component in 12 of this total and in 6 of the G7 countries.

Presentation

In addition to index descriptions and tabular material, profiles of the index capitalisation (or the market capitalisation), usually for 1990 and 1995, are provided where available, detailing weights by company or sector. This is intended to show where there may be a relative dominance and thus where there may be a possible sensitivity of the total index to the fortunes of that dominant player. Of interest is the fact that in some countries additional indices are compiled in which the weighting of such dominant players is restricted to a specific level.

Share Selection and Weighting

There is a marked degree of uniformity in the bases from which shares are selected and in the compilation of the indices. It seems appropriate, therefore, to describe these uniform elements here, rather than in each country section.

In the majority of cases, the shares used in the compilations are either all or a sample of those traded on the 'Official' or 'First' section of an exchange. Exchanges are usually structured into first and subsidiary sections, with the first section restricted to shares meeting admission criteria which include documented profit earning capability; specified standards of financial control, shareholder base, market value and turnover; accessibility of the general public to the shares of the company; etc. When a sample approach is used, the selection is made to reflect as closely as possible the market as a whole and often will represent a significant percentage of the market's capitalisation. In other cases, the index may be one of the top, say, 100 companies but the selected companies again represent almost the total market capitalisation. In a few instances, all companies may be used in the compilations, but with exclusions relating to a lack of turnover, etc.

As noted above, the criteria for admission to the first section of an exchange often result in the exclusion of companies whose shares are not easily accessible to the general public. (Other terms used here include 'freely transferable', 'deliverable' etc.). In most cases when a company with major blocks of shares unavailable to the public meets the admission criteria, then all shares are considered for the compilation. Occasionally, however, the index authorities will construct the index on only those shares which are deliverable, either by weighting adjustment factors or by considering only the deliverable shares.

A further similarity relates to weighting. The weighting of the different share price increases used in the compilations is invariably by market capitalisation. In its simplest form the index can be said to measure the current aggregated market value (i.e. the sum of the products of outstanding shares multiplied by current prices) of the stocks included in the index as a proportion of the base aggregated market value (i.e. sum of the products of outstanding shares multiplied by the base prices).

Additionally, the aggregated market values are nearly always obtained as arithmetic weighted averages of the price movements of the index components. Only the Czech Republic differs in this regard by employing a geometric weighted average.

Additional Factors

Other main choices are in the shares types and in the prices to be used in the calculation -- are the shares to be restricted to common/ordinary shares; is the price the last available quotation or is it restricted to that involving a specified volume or is it to be an average of prices relating to different 'lots' in which the share may be traded; etc? In general, the shares used are common shares, while the price used is the last available quotation, not limited to specified volumes or averages thereof.

Mention should perhaps here be made of the fact that a number of influences can bear on the price of a share, and thus the index, without having a direct relation to the underlying valuation of the company concerned. Most noticeable is the impact that dividend payments make on a share's price. The price of a company's stock increases as the date of a dividend payment approaches and drops to its ex-dividend level immediately after the dividend payment is made. Some exchanges make no adjustment to eliminate this variation, while others do. When an adjustment is made, it is usually by way of estimates designed to reduce the traded price to a lower ex-dividend level, i.e. to one excluding the price increase prior to the dividend payment date and the price fall at this date.

Capital Changes

An additional similarity of approach by the index authorities can be noticed in the methods employed to accommodate recurring capital changes. Such changes impact on capitalisation values but are not related to price variations associated with market trading. Adjustments are introduced to ensure the index remains unaltered following these changes. When these adjustments are incorporated, they nearly all involve adjustments to the base, defined as the base year or the previously constructed index level, either through the embodiment of an adjustment factor in the formula employed in the construction of the index or through a simple alteration of the base value proportional to the change in the current market capitalisation. As a consequence of this, the above equation may now be modified to read 'The index measures the current aggregated market value of the stocks included in the index as a proportion of a comparable base aggregated market value for such stocks'.

With regard to these capital changes, the case of a rights issue to shareholders of record is given as an example. Such an issue occurs when a company offers its shareholders of record the right to buy, at a preferential price, one new share for each of a specified number of shares held. The day the stock sells 'ex-rights', the additional shares together with the original shares represent the number of shares outstanding, but all are now priced at a lower level that results from the fact that the 'rights' component of the total was sold at a preferential, i.e. discounted price. The aggregated base market value is adjusted, by taking into account both the market price and the subscription price, in order to eliminate the variation that would otherwise result. In practice, indices often include shares to be issued under a rights issue when the announcement is made, since to do otherwise is difficult from a calculation viewpoint.

Other events generally resulting in a change in capital include:

- issue or withdrawal of shares (shares issued for takeovers or additional shares of an index stock through subscription rights / private placement/ public offering, conversion of convertible bonds or convertible preferred stock into common stock, purchase or retirement of company's own stock, etc.)
- bankruptcy or liquidation, new constituent company, take-overs and mergers, delisting etc.
- asset spin-off (share value decreases after a company disposes of some of its asset base)
- control block adjustment (for indices where only publicly accessible shares are considered)

Events generally not requiring adjustment are those which do not result in a change in capital. They can include dividends issued in the form of additional stock, where the price of the stock should drop to the extent of the worth of the dividend. Similarly, in the case of share splits, the increased number of shares times the resulting lower price should equal the old number of shares times the previous higher price. In the case of stock consolidations, the higher price times the smaller number of shares should leave the current aggregate market value unchanged.

However, there is not a total uniformity in the way these events are treated. It is for this reason that the caveat 'generally' was employed in the preceding paragraphs. Occasionally, for example, the index compilers do not accept the assumption that share splits result in no change in capitalisation, in which case an adjustment is made to the base value after a determination of the actual post-split value of the shares in question.

Overview

Finally a brief, non-exhaustive overview is given of a number of influences that can bear on a share price index, some of which will obviously detract from its use as an economic activity indicator, while others will help to explain why the index level is where it is. They are offered as additional information which may help provide a better insight into the subject of share price indices but also to highlight the caution that is necessarily required in any international comparison of the indices. Although stress has been made of the similarities that exist, the fact still remains that these indices are very disparate things.

Regarding possible drawbacks of the indices as indicators. Within some countries, a significant element of the economy may rest in companies for which there are no publicly offered shares. Such companies could be a) small in scale, perhaps family controlled, but sharing the characteristic of relying on borrowing for their capital needs, b) large state-owned enterprises or c) subsidiaries of overseas companies. Or again the index may not reflect the actual economy if capitalization is dominated by certain sectors, for example the utility industry, while say construction, perhaps contributing as much to the economy, has a low capitalization.

Actions by companies in the form of stock buy backs and company mergers help shrink the number of shares available. Investment monies chase fewer opportunities, a competitive process can emerge and share prices can rise. The index may register a movement but it could be inappropriate to associate this with a change in the economic climate.

Movements in foreign exchange rates can exert an appreciable influence on an index when, for example, an economy highly reliant on exports experiences a strengthening of its national currency, thus raising the price of its exported products. As a consequence there will be diminished interest in the shares of the exporting companies.

Institutional factors can play a role. If there are constraints on foreign ownership -- either legislated or via taxes on capital transfers, stamp duties, punitive and/or discriminatory capital gains taxes where no bilateral treaties exist, etc. -- there will be less competition for shares offered and the index will be lower than otherwise. Additionally, governments may limit share price variations, for example by precluding a price change of more than, say, 5% from a previous day's closing. This would be a temporary measure aimed at allowing an orderly maturing of an infant exchange.

What of the Future?

Will indices continue to play a significant role as economic activity indicators? As movement towards liberalization and harmonization of stock exchange activity gains momentum, trading in London may influence, say, the opening trading of the Tokyo exchange and thus the Tokyo index. Such price changes are still the result of a change in investors' views. However, this development of having a company's stock traded on more than one exchange may well mean that the index for a country's exchange is increasingly less reflective of that domestic economy, given the inclusion of foreign stock. Another development could be the possibility of smaller exchanges being forced out of business as the more successful, bigger exchanges enjoy an increasing share of a global market in security trading. One viewpoint of this development may be that integration of exchange activity is proceeding alongside the integration of national economies and that each of the surviving indices could reflect to a certain degree a number of individual national economies. Or again, additional new indices may be compiled that relate not to specific exchanges as such, but to specific economies, with the basic information being obtained from more than one exchange. Such a development would involve the conversion, through the use of exchange rates, of the basic information from the national currency (on which the exchange specific indices are presently constructed) into a standard currency, say the U.S. dollar. It is interesting to note that some 'combined' indices are already being computed, e.g. the FTSE International World Indices. Given that in some countries, overseas investment in certain companies is limited to specific levels, the weighting for these companies in the World Indices is restricted to correspond to the permitted maximum overseas investment.

2. Explanatory notes

Most OECD Sources and Methods publications are structured according to a standard list of metadata items (detailed below). However, for both share price indices and interest rates this structure is not entirely relevant. For those categories which are not relevant, titles do not appear in the text. In other instances, where it was deemed appropriate, categories have been amalgamated.

METADATA ITEMS

SOURCE

- **Source agencies**
- **Key national publication sources**
- **Series title in national publications**
- **Breakdown available**
- **Methodological references**
- **Run of data available**
- **Periodicity**
- **Unit of measurement**

CONCEPTS AND COVERAGE

- **Definition**
- **Coverage**
  - Reference period
  - Geographical coverage
  - Statistical population
  - Classification coverage
  - Particular exclusions

STANDARDS

- **Standard systems / framework**
- **Standard classifications / nomenclatures**
- **International comparability**
- **Departures from international standards**

DATA COLLECTION

- **Reporting units**
- **Reporting method**
- **Survey details**
  - Description of questionnaire
  - Master list
  - Survey description
  - Non-response rate

DATA COLLECTION (continued)

- **Administrative source details**
  - Description
  - Update procedures
  - Quality assessment
  - Access and control for statistical usage
  - Statistical techniques for processing data
- **Multiple source details**
  - Description
  - Standard combination framework
  - Statistical techniques for combining multiple sources
- **Reporting date in relation to the event measured**
- **Time lapse between event and processing**

DATA MANIPULATION

- **Aggregation / Grossing up**
  - Grossing up method
  - Aggregation method
  - Weights for aggregation
- **Seasonal and other adjustments**
- **Other manipulations**

DATA QUALITY AND TIMELINESS

- **Sampling errors and their corrections**
- **Other errors and their corrections**
- **Missing data in time series**
- **Breaks in time series**
- **Preliminary estimates**
- **Revision policy**
- **Corroborating data**
- **Timeliness**
- **Release dates**

A. INTEREST RATES

CANADA

(a) Official discount % pa

Definition: The Bank Rate is the minimum rate at which the Bank of Canada makes short-term advances to the chartered banks and the other members of the Canadian Payments Association. Since the 13 March 1980, the rate has been set at 1/4 % above the weekly average tender rate on 3-month treasury bills.

Reference period: Data refer to rate applying at end of period.

(b) Money market % pa

Definition: Day-to-day loans are made by the chartered banks to those money market dealers who have pre-arranged lines of credit with the Bank of Canada. Collateral for these loans consists of money market instruments -- Government of Canada Treasury bills and short-term Government of Canada direct and guaranteed securities. These loans may be made at any time and access of the dealers to the Bank of Canada as a lender of last resort ensures their liquidity. If an approved money market dealer cannot obtain day money from the banks, he can sell market securities directly to the Bank with a purchase and resale agreement (PRA). The data shown exclude such PRAs and day-to-day loans between banks.

Reference period: Data refer to the 7 day average of the week ending with the last Wednesday of the period.

(c) 90 day deposit receipts % pa

Definition: Data refer to rates on bankers' acceptances of 90-day deposits and are calculated as weighted averages of mid-market closing rates for typical quotes.

Reference period: Prior to April 1981, data refer to the last Wednesday of the month. Thereafter, the rate shown is the monthly average of Wednesday rates. Annual and quarterly data are averages of monthly figures.

(d) Yield on government bonds % pa

Definition: Data refer to an unweighted arithmetic average of the yield in the secondary market on Government of Canada outstanding issues with a remaining term to maturity of more than 10 years. All direct marketable debt payable in Canadian dollars is used for the averages, with the exception of guaranteed issues such as Canada Savings bonds. The quotes used are the mid-points between bid and asked prices in the bond market at the close of business on Wednesdays.

Reference period: Since April 1981, the rate shown is the monthly average of Wednesday rates. Annual and quarterly data are averages of monthly figures.

(e) Prime paper % pa

Definition: The rate shown is the Bank of Canada's estimate of operative trading levels for major borrowers' paper and here refers to 90 day corporate paper.

Reference period: Monthly data refer to the last Wednesday of the period. Quarterly and annual data are averages of monthly data.

(f) Prime interest rate % pa

Definition: The rate shown is the chartered banks' rate on prime business loans charged to the most creditworthy borrowers. It is the rate applying to large business loans.

Reference period: Data refer to the last Wednesday of the period.

MEXICO

(a) 3-month CETES % pa

Definition: The 3-month CETES (Certificado de Tesoreria) rate is the monthly average rate of 3-month Federal Treasury bills. (Returns are tax exempt).

Reference period: Data are calculated as averages of daily quotations.

UNITED STATES

(a) Federal Funds rate % pa

Definition: Federal funds are balances available immediately rather than on the following business day. They are borrowed or lent by commercial banks and others to adjust reserve positions or make payments on a day-to-day basis. The effective rate on these Federal funds is estimated daily by the Federal Reserve Bank of New York and is a weighted average of rates on trades through New York brokers.

Reference period: Monthly data are averages of daily rates, while quarterly and annual data relate to the final monthly figure of the period.

(b) Prime interest rate % pa

Definition: The prime rate is the rate that banks charge their most credit-worthy business customers on short-term loans and is the base from which rates charged on loans to other business customers are scaled upwards. Prime rates are formally posted only by the largest banks. Daily rates are developed from rates charged by some thirty large commercial banks. The daily figure is not an average, but that rate charged by a majority of the banks surveyed.

Reference period: Monthly data are averages of daily rates, while quarterly and annual data relate to the final monthly figure of the period.

(c) Certificates of deposit % pa

Definition: The rate is that for large negotiable certificates of deposit (3-month) issued by commercial banks and is the unweighted average of offered rates quoted by five or more dealers in the secondary market.

Reference period: Data are averages of daily rates.

(d) Government bonds: yield % pa

Definition: This composite rate relates to yields on the secondary market on a varying number of United States government bonds maturing or callable in 10 or more years. Daily rates are calculated as unweighted averages, computed from closing bid prices.

Reference period: Data are averages of daily rates.

AUSTRALIA

(a) Bank-accepted bills (90 days) % pa

Definition: The series relate to the purchases of bank-accepted commercial bills in the commercial bill market. The yields are based on information obtained by the Reserve Bank from authorised short-term money market dealers.

Reference period: Monthly data refer to the arithmetic averages of yields on each of the working days of the week ending the last Wednesday of the month. Annual and quarterly data are averages of monthly figures.

(b) Long-term Treasury bonds % pa

Definition: Data refer to the estimated closing yields on Commonwealth Government bonds with maturities of 10 years. The estimates are based primarily on information reported by bond dealers in secondary market trading.

Reference period: Monthly data relate to the last business day of the month. Annual and quarterly data are averages of monthly figures.

JAPAN

(a) Official discount % pa

Definition: The official discount rate is regarded as the base rate and is the discount rate on commercial bills and the interest rate on loans secured by government bonds, specially designated securities and bills corresponding to commercial bills. Apart from banks, other financial institutions may borrow from the Bank of Japan. These include credit associations, co-operatives, securities finance companies, call loan dealers, large securities companies and resident foreign banks.

Reference period: Data refer to the end of period.

(b) Call money % pa

Definition: The call money market allows certain institutions, unable fully to meet their customers' requirements from their own funds and deposits, to borrow from other institutions with surpluses. The overnight uncollateralised call rate is the median rate on the largest volumes of transactions each day.

Reference period: Monthly data are arithmetic averages of daily rates. Quarterly and annual data are the rate shown for the last month of the period.

(c) Certificates of deposit % pa

Definition: Data are average interest rates on 3-month certificates of deposit of city banks, long-term credit banks and trust banks. These certificates are large negotiable CDs sold chiefly to non-financial enterprises and local governments.

Reference period: Data are averages of daily rates.

(d) Bond yields: central gvt. % pa

Definition: All long-term Central Government bond issues are listed on the stock exchange in the month following the first interest payment. Data refer to this secondary market yield on 10-year bonds.

Reference period: Monthly data are end of month rates. Quarterly and annual data are averages of monthly figures.

KOREA

(a) Interbank transactions % pa

Definition: The interbank transactions call rate is the interest charged on overnight loans among banks and between banks and other financial institutions. These loans are subject to call thereafter. The Bank of Korea collects the relevant information on these interbank loans daily from investment and finance companies. The daily rate is an average weighted by transaction amounts.

Reference period: Monthly data are averages of daily rates. Annual and quarterly data refer to the final month of the period.

(b) 3-month deposits % pa

Definition: The rate on traded certificates of deposit is the 91-day rate on the primary and secondary markets. The daily rate is obtained as a simple average yield of the ten largest securites companies when their final selling prices are not equal. However, when the final selling price of at least five of these companies is equal, then the daily rate is obtained as a yield based on this price.

Reference period: Data are averages of daily rates.

(c) Yield of 5 year bonds % pa

Definition: Data measure yields on traded 5-year National Housing Bonds 'type 1', one of a number of government bonds. The daily rate is obtained as the simple average yield of the ten largest securities companies when their final selling prices are not equal. However, when the final selling price of at least five of these companies is equal, then the daily rate is obtained as a yield based on this price.

Reference period: Data are averages of daily rates.

NEW ZEALAND

(a) Bank bills (90 days) % pa

Definition: Data refer to the average of market rates at 11 a.m. each day for bank bills with approximately 90 days to maturity.

Reference period: Data are averages of daily rates.

(b) Yield of government bonds % pa

Definition: Data refer to the yield of 10-year government bonds on the secondary market. The 10-year benchmark was the 15 April 2004 bond for the period 1 July 1993 to 4 July 1995. The current benchmark is the 15 November 2006 bond.

Reference period: Monthly data are end of month rates, while quarterly and annual data are averages of monthly figures.

AUSTRIA

(a) Official discount % pa

Definition: The official discount rate is the rate at which, for selected banks, the National Bank of Austria rediscounts bills of exchange. To qualify for discounting the paper presented must fulfil certain eligibility requirements. Changes in this rate are an indicator of the Bank's monetary policy and are generally followed by credit rates charged by commercial banks to borrowers.

Reference period: Data refer to end of period.

(b) 3-month VIBOR % pa

Definition: The 3-month VIBOR (Vienna Interbank Offered Rate) for variable-rate Treasury bills is used as a reference rate for 3-month loans between banks for any excess or shortage of liquidity over several months. The rate is determined daily on the basis of selling rates reported by selected banks in Vienna.

Reference period: Data are averages of daily rates.

(c) Yield of public sector bonds % pa

Definition: The yield relates to the secondary market yield on bonds outstanding with a maturity of more than one year.

Reference period: Data are averages of daily rates.

BELGIUM

(a) Central Bank rate % pa

Definition: The Central Bank rate is the rate at which the National Bank of Belgium makes advances to financial intermediaries to meet daily deficits.

Reference period: Monthly data are averages of daily rates. Annual and quarterly data refer to the final month of the period.

(b) Treasury certificates % pa

Definition: Data refer to the tender rate on 3-month Treasury certificates. Prior to 1991, figures refer to the rate at issue.

Reference period: Data are averages of daily rates.

c) Yield of government bonds % pa

Definition: Data refer to the yield on government bonds (6-years and over) in the secondary market.

Reference period: Data are averages of daily rates.

CZECH REPUBLIC

(a) Official discount % pa

Definition: The official discount rate is the rate at which the Central Bank lends to commercial banks.

Reference period: Data refer to end of period.

(b) 3-month PRIBOR % pa

Definition: Data refer to the 3-month Prague Interbank Offered Rate.

Reference period: Data are averages of daily rates.

DENMARK

(a) Official discount % pa

Definition: The official discount rate is charged for drawings against the first tranche of bank loans from the Central Bank. The charge for drawings against the second tranche is the official discount rate plus 3 percentage points.

Reference period: Data refer to end of period.

(b) 3-month interbank rate % pa

Definition: Data refer to the 3-month Danish interbank rate.

Reference period: Monthly data are end of period. Annual and quarterly data are averages of monthly figures.

(c) Yield of 10-yr gvt. bonds % pa

Definition: The rate given is a weighted average of rates of yield on 10-year Central Government bonds for which the nominal interest rate equals 7% or more.

Reference period: Monthly data refer to end of period. Annual and quarterly data are averages of monthly figures.

FINLAND

(a) Base rate % pa

Definition: The base rate, formerly the official discount rate, is fixed by the Bank of Finland and is the rate to which other rates are more or less linked, particularly those relating to the household sector.

Reference period: Data refer to end of period.

(b) Liquidity credit rate % pa

Definition: Those credit institutions subject to the minimum reserve requirement and maintaining a current account with the Bank of Finland may obtain liquidity credit to cover overdrafts and to fulfil their minimum reserve requirment. Such credit has a maturity of one, seven, fourteen, twenty-one or twenty-eight days, with the actual maturity being determined by the Bank. The rate of interest on liquidity credit is obtained by adding together the Bank of Finland's Tender rate and the interest rate margin for liquidity credit. (The Tender rate is determined in tenders held by the Bank in which banks are asked to make bids or offers for money market instruments with a maturity of one month and is a weighted average of accepted bids or offers).

Reference period: Data refer to end of period.

(c) 3-month HELIBOR % pa

Definition: Data refer to the 3-month Helsinki Interbank Offered Rate. Since June 1995, the rate has been calculated on the basis of the bid rates (offered rates for funds) quoted for their certificates of deposit by all banks accepted by the Bank of Finland as counterparts in money market operations.

Reference period: Data are averages of daily rates.

(d) Yield of public bonds % pa

Definition: Data refer to the rate of interest on taxable public issues and is the effective annual yield in the secondary market, calculated as the arithmetic mean, on fixed rate government bonds with a remaining maturity of between three and six years.

Reference period: Data are averages of daily rates.

FRANCE

(a) Call money % pa

Definition: Data refer to rate on call money loans. The Bank of France computes an average rate on overnight lending against bills, weighted according to the amount of transactions.

Reference period: Monthly figures are arithmetic averages of the calculated daily figures. Annual and quarterly data refer to the final month of the period.

(b) Bond yields: gvt. guaranteed % pa

Definition: Government guaranteed bond yield is an average of yield measured at time of payment for bonds issued during the month. In practice, these bonds are public sector bonds, excluding those of the central government. As each issue is distinct from other issues, primary market yields can be analysed by calculating the average (weighted) yields of issues over the period. Only those issues above a specified limit are accounted for, with the limit itself revised periodically.

Reference period: Monthly data are as defined above. Annual and quarterly data refer to the average of monthly data.

(c) Bond yields: not guaranteed % pa

Definition: In practice, the yield relates to bonds issued by the private sector and is calculated as defined in b) above.

Reference period: See b) above.

(d) 3-month PIBOR % pa

Definition: Data refer to the 3-month Paris Interbank Offered Rate. It is calculated as an arithmetic average of rates provided by eight representative institutions and after the four highest and lowest rates have been eliminated.

Reference period: Data are averages of daily rates.

(e) Bonds: public and semi-public % pa

Definition: Data refer to the yields paid on long-term public and semi-public bonds on the secondary market. From January 1988, data are based on a sample of bonds not subject to tax credit.

Reference period: Monthly data refer to the last Friday of the month. Annual and quarterly data are averages of monthly data.

GERMANY

(a) Official discount % pa

Definition: The official discount rate is the rate of interest at which the Bundesbank discounts eligible commercial paper within the limits of 'rediscount quotas' prescribed by it. Eligible commercial paper is bills of exchange backed by solvent parties and payable within three months of the date of purchase by the Bundesbank. Data refer to unified Germany from July 1990 and western Germany prior to this date.

Reference period: Data refer to end of period

(b) Call money % pa

Definition: Day-to-day money is interbank money mostly lent or borrowed without security to meet temporary excesses or shortages of liquidity. The Bundesbank itself engages in money market operations in order to influence the call money rate through repurchase agreements in eligible bonds, etc. Data refer to unified Germany from July 1990 and western Germany prior to this date.

Reference period: Monthly data are unweighted averages of daily returns in the Frankfurt market. Annual and quarterly data refer to the final month of the period.

(c) 3-month FIBOR % pa

Definition: The 3-month Frankfurt Interbank Offered Rate relates to loans given or taken amongst banks to meet an excess or shortage of liquidity over several months. It is taken as a reference rate for variable rate bonds. Data refer to unified Germany from July 1990 and western Germany prior to this date.

Reference period: Data are unweighted averages of daily rates.

(d) Public sector bond yield % pa

Definition: The public sector bond yield refers to long-term bonds (7 to 10 years' duration) on the secondary market. Data refer to unified Germany from July 1990 and western Germany prior to this date.

Reference period: Data are averages of daily rates.

GREECE

(a) Overnight interbank rate % pa

Definition: The overnight interbank rate relates to loans for a one-night period.

Reference period: Data refer to end of period.

(b) 12-month Treasury bills % pa

Definition: Data refer to the rate on 12-month treasury bills.

Reference period: Data are averages of daily rates.

HUNGARY

(a) Official discount % pa

Definition: Data refer to the basic rate on refinancing credit maturing over one year that the Central Bank lends to financial institutions.

Reference period: Data refer to end of period.

(b) Call money % pa

Definition: Data refer to the interbank money market rate on credit for two days or less.

Reference period: Monthly data are averages of daily rates. Annual and quarterly data refer to the final month of the period.

(c) Treasury bills (90 days) % pa

Definition: Data refer to the yields observed at the bi-monthly auctions of 90-day treasury bills.

Reference period: Data are averages of daily rates.

ICELAND

(a) Treasury bills (90 days) % pa

Definition: Data refer to the rate on 90-day treasury bills. From January 1988 to October 1992, data refer to 'sales on tap, large quantity purchases', and from November 1992 to 'auctioned primary issues'.

Reference period: Monthly data refer to end of period, while annual and quarterly figures are averages of monthly data.

(b) Indexed 10-year government bonds % pa

Definition: Data refer to real yields on indexed 10-year government bonds.

Reference period: Monthly data refer to end of period, while annual and quarterly figures are averages of monthly data.

IRELAND

(a) Call money % pa

Definition: Call money interbank overnight market rates are average dealing rates based on data supplied by the financial institutions operating in the market.

Reference period: Data refer to end of period.

(b) 3-month interbank rate % pa

Definition: The 3-month interbank rate (Dublin) refers to average dealing rates based on data supplied by the financial institutions operating in the market.

Reference period: Monthly rates relate to those prevailing on the last day of each month. (Prior to January 1990, they relate to those on the last Friday in the month). Annual and quarterly data are averages of monthly figures.

(c) Yield of government bonds % pa

Definition: The yield shown is a representative yield on long-term government bonds of 15 years to maturity.

Reference period: Monthly data refer to the last Friday of the month. Annual and quarterly data are averages of monthly figures.

(d) Short-term facility (STF) % pa

Definition: The STF is the rate set by the central bank at which credit institutions can borrow Irish pounds from the bank on an overnight basis against approved security. The rate charged for STF funds is the key official interest rate and in normal circumstances sets the upper limit for wholesale money-market rates.

Reference period: Data refer to end of period.

ITALY

(a) Official discount % pa

Definition: The official discount rate is the rate at which the Bank of Italy discounts bills for the commercial banks.

Reference period: Data refer to end of period.

(b) 3-month interbank deposits % pa

Definition: The rate is the rate that applies on 3-month interbank sight deposits on amounts of one billion lira or more. Daily rates are the averages of transaction rates, weighted by the amounts transacted.

Reference period: Data are averages of daily rates.

(c) Long-term treasury bonds % pa

Definition: Data refer to the secondary market yield of treasury bonds with a maturity of one year or more. Daily rates are obtained from stock exchange quotes.

Reference period: Data are averages of daily rates.

(d) Bond yield % pa

Definition: Data relate to the expected average yield to redemption on a sample of bonds most frequently traded on the secondary market.

Reference period: Data refer to the arithmetic average of daily stock exchange prices.

LUXEMBOURG

(a) Minimum mortgage interest rate % pa

Definition: Data refer to the minimum interest rate granted by credit institutions for mortgage loans.

Reference period: Annual and quarterly data relate to the final month of the period.

(b) Bond yield % pa

Definition: Data refer to the yield of 5 to 10 year non-government bonds.

Reference period: Monthly data refer to the yield applicable at the beginning of the month. Annual and quarterly data relate to the average of monthly data.

NETHERLANDS

(a) Call money (Amsterdam) % pa

Definition: Data refer to the rate on unsecured call loans between banks.

Reference period: Monthly data are unweighted averages of representative daily rates, while annual and quarterly data relate to the final month of the period.

(b) 3-month AIBOR % pa

Definition: This is the rate applying to Amsterdam Interbank Offered Rate on 3-month loans, calculated on the basis of interbank rates offered by eight banks.

Reference period: Data are averages of daily rates.

(c) Yield of government bonds % pa

Definition: Data refer to the yield on the five longest term central government bonds.

Reference period: Data are the weighted average of the true yield to maturity of each of the five bonds, the weights based on the remaining outstanding nominal value of the bonds.

NORWAY

(a) Call money % pa

Definition: Redistribution of liquidity between the largest Norwegian banks usually takes place in a market for currency swaps. The euro-krone interest rates in this market are based on forward and spot-exchange rates on US-dollar and euro-dollar interest rates.

Reference period: Monthly data are averages of daily rates. Annual and quarterly data refer to the final month of the period.

(b) 3-month NIBOR % pa

Definition: 3-month NIBOR are euro-krone interest rates based on quoted selling rates for five large banks.

Reference period: Data are averages of daily rates.

(c) Yield of government bonds % pa

Definition: Data refer to the yield on the secondary market of central government bonds with average expected remaining maturity of 6 to 10 years.

Reference period: Data are averages of daily rates.

POLAND

(a) Official discount % pa

Definition: The official discount rate refers to the end of period refinancing rate. It is the annual rate offered to commercial banks by the Bank of Poland.

Reference period: Data, including monthly, refer to end of period.

(b) 3-month Treasury bills % pa

Definition: Data refer to the yield on 13-week treasury bills.

Reference period: Data are averages of daily rates.

PORTUGAL

(a) 86-96 day interbank rate % pa

Definition: Data relate to interbank loans of 86-96 day duration.

Reference period: Monthly data are averages of daily rates, weighted by the amounts involved. Annual and quarterly data are averages of monthly figures.

(b) 91-day Treasury bills % pa

Definition: Data refer to the rate on 91-day treasury bills on the primary market. From 4 May 1989, figures are the gross interest rate (before tax).

Reference period: Monthly data are the average of daily allotment rates weighted by the amounts involved, but excluding purchases by the Bank of Portugal. Annual and quarterly data are averages of monthly figures.

(c) Yield of government bonds % pa

Definition: Data refer to the yield on 10-year government debt bonds on the secondary market.

Reference period: Monthly data are weighted averages of daily figures. (If on a particular day no trade occurs on this maturity, the yield on the bond with the longest maturity is taken). Annual and quarterly data are averages of monthly figures.

SPAIN

(a) Call money % pa

Definition: The rate shown relates to interbank day-to-day loans. The daily rate is an average weighted by the amount of credit granted.

Reference period: Monthly data refer to the arithmetic average of daily rates. Annual and quarterly data refer to the final month of the period.

(b) 3-month interbank loans % pa

Definition: The rate shown relates to interbank 3-month loans. The daily rate is an average weighted by the amount of credit granted.

Reference period: Data are averages of daily rates.

(b) Long-term government bonds % pa

Definition: Data relate to the yield of government bonds of more than two years on the secondary market. Daily yields are obtained by weighting the yields of each operation according to the amounts traded.

Reference period: Data are averages of daily rates.

SWEDEN

(a) Official discount % pa

Definition: The official discount rate is established by the central bank but is now significant only in administrative matters, exerting little influence on other rates. It is determined at the beginning of each quarter and is based on rates prevailing in the preceding quarter. It is calculated as a weighted average of daily rates for T-bills of 6 months to 5 years, less two and a half percentage points.

Reference period: Data refer to end of period.

(b) Treasury discount notes % pa

Definition: Data refer to the effective rate of 3-month treasury discount notes.

Reference period: Data are averages of daily rates.

(c) Yield long-term gvt. bonds % pa

Definition: Data refer to the yield in the secondary market on 10-year government bonds

Reference period: Data are averages of daily rates.

SWITZERLAND

(a) Official discount % pa

Definition: The official discount rate is a weighted average of the volumes of securities which the Swiss National Bank actually discounts. The Bank is authorised to discount such paper but is not obliged to do so. Any paper discounted must be of a limited maturity, must be commercial and not financial paper, and must be guaranteed by signatures of accepted solvency.

Reference period: Data refer to end of period.

(b) Call money (Zurich) % pa

Definition: The call money rate is the interest rate charged by banks on the sums they lend for twenty-four hour periods.

Reference period: Monthly data are averages of daily rates, while annual and quarterly data refer to the final month of the period.

(c) 3-month Euro-deposits % pa

Definition: Data refer to the rate paid on the Euro-money market on 3-month deposits.

Reference period: Data are averages of daily rates.

(d) Yield of bonds % pa

Definition: Data refer to the average yield on Confederation bonds. The lower of the following two rates is shown. One calculation is based on the date of the final repayment of the bond, while the other relies on the next date for early repayment. The latter is often invoked by the issuer to minimise interest payments.

Reference period: Data are averages of daily rates.

TURKEY

(a) Overnight Interbank Rate % pa

Definition: Data refer to the rate charged on overnight interbank transactions. The daily rate is an average weighted by amounts transacted.

Reference period: Monthly data are averages of daily rates, weighted by amounts transacted. Annual and quarterly data refer to the final month of the period.

(b) 6-month Treasury bills % pa

Definition: The annual simple interest rate of government bills auctioned with a 6-month term (or a close approximation in days).

Reference period: Monthly data are last quoted interest rate in month. Annual and quarterly data are averages of monthly figures.

UNITED KINGDOM

(a) Overnight interbank rate % pa

Definition: The overnight interbank rate relates to loans for a one-night period.

Reference period: Monthly data are averages of daily rates. Annual and quarterly data refer to the final month of the period.

(b) London clearing banks' base rate % pa

Definition: Data are based on rates set by the major commercial banks for loans advanced by these banks to discount houses.

Reference period: Data refer to end of period.

(c) 3-month interbank loans % pa

Definition: Data refer to rates on 3-month interbank loans. Daily rates are established as the mid-point between bid and offered rates at a specific time each day.

Reference period: Data are averages of daily rates.

(d) Yield of long-term gvt. bonds % pa

Definition: Data refer to the par yield of central government bonds maturing in 10 years. A par yield is the interest rate (coupon) which a hypothetical stock would have to bear for its price to equal its face value. The par yield for any maturity is generated by a mathematical model which, using only conventional dated stocks with a signifiant amount in issue, plots a yield curve of observed maturities (1 year to over 20 years).

Reference period: Data are averages of daily rates.

B. SHARE PRICES

Index Characteristics

Y = Yes
N = No

	Index excludes			Share Selection Restricted to		Traded price adjusted to eliminate price variation associated with dividend payments
	a Foreign Companies	b Units of Investment/ Mutual Funds	c Holding Companies	a 'Ordinary type' equity issues	b Publicly accessible	
1. Canada	Y	Y	N	Y	Y	Y[2]
2. Mexico			Y		N	N
3. United States	N	N		Y	N	N
4. Australia				Y	Y	N
5. Japan	Y	Y		Y	Y[1]	N
6. Korea						
7. New Zealand				Y		N
8. Austria	Y	Y	Y	N	Y[1]	N
9. Belgium	Y	Y		N	N	N
10. Czech Republic	Y	N	Y	Y	Y	Y
11. Denmark	Y	Y	Y	N	N	Y
12. Finland	N	Y		N	Y	
13. France		Y			N	N
14. Germany	Y	Y	N	N[3]	Y	N
15. Greece				N	N	N
16. Iceland						
17. Ireland		Y		Y	N	N
18. Italy	N	Y	N	N	N	Y
19. Netherlands	Y	Y	Y	Y	N	N
20. Norway	Y			N	Y	Y
21. Poland	Y	Y	N			N
22. Portugal	N	Y	Y	Y	Y[1]	Y
23. Spain	Y	Y				Y
24. Sweden	N			N	Y[1]	N
25. Switzerland				N		N
26. Turkey		Y		Y	Y	N
27. United Kingdom				Y	Y[1]	N

(1) Companies with non-transferable blocks are excluded from the index constituents if they fail to meet the admission criteria regarding 'deliverable' shares. If they meet the criteria, all shares are considered in the index calculation.
(2) Adjustments are made to traded prices when cash dividends (together with stock dividends and rights issues) exceed a specified limit.
(3) Ordinary and preferred (no voting rights) shares.

CANADA

Title in Publication

The TSE 300 Composite Index

CONCEPTS AND COVERAGE

Definition

The Toronto Stock Exchange (TSE) 300 Composite index is a price index, created and maintained by the exchange, as a measure of the performance of the broad Canadian equity market. It covers the top 300 shares in terms of float market capitalisation of those listed as eligible for inclusion in the index.

Coverage

All classes of common shares, issued and outstanding, are considered. If a company has more than one class of common share, each share is considered independently. With few exceptions preferred shares are not included, nor are Limited Partnerships, Royalty Trusts, etc.

To be considered for inclusion in the index, companies must have been listed on the exchange for at least one year, or for at least six months if they rank in the top 150 in terms of float market capitalisation. Trading volume of stock in the 12 month period immediately preceding consideration must be at least 100,000 shares and 100 transactions, with a trading value in excess of $1,000,000. Stocks matching these criteria are ranked according to their one-year average 'float' quoted market value. This 'float' is determined by removing major shareholders defined as individual or related groups of shareholders which in aggregate total 20% or more of the total number of shares issued and outstanding. The market value is derived by multiplying the one-year trade-weighted average price of the stock for the preceding twelve-month period by its float outstanding at the end of this period.

The top 300 stocks determined in this annual review process are the constituents of the TSE 300 Composite Index, the remainder forming a pool of eligible replacement stocks for the subsequent twelve month period. Such replacements occur when take-overs, mergers, bankruptcies, asset spin-offs or other corporate actions reduce the number of constituents to fewer than 300.

% Weighting and Number of Components

	1990		1995	
	%	No.	%	No.
Metals and Minerals	8.06	18	9.21	11
Gold and Precious Minerals	9.60	34	10.60	27
Oil and Gas	8.77	34	12.24	59
Consumer Products	7.99	25	6.85	20
Industrial Products	9.85	35	16.29	49
Utilities	11.39	16	8.87	21
Financial Services	18.76	36	15.70	26
All Other	25.58	102	20.24	87
Total	100.00	300	100.00	300

SOURCE

Source Agencies

The TSE compiles and disseminates the index which is also re-published by the Bank of Canada.

Key national publication sources

The publication source is: Bank of Canada Review, Table F3, Stock Market Statistics, Toronto Stock Exchange, stock price indexes, composite, close.

Breakdown available/ Other related indices

Sub-indices are computed and published relating to sectors such as Oil and Gas, Metals and Minerals, Utilities, Paper and Forest Products, Financial Services, etc. A still more restricted index, the Toronto 35 Index, is also published by the TSE. Indices relating to the Montreal Stock Exchange, including the Canadian Market Portfolio (25) and Banks (6), are available from the Montreal exchange.

Methodological references

A publicly available article produced by the Toronto exchange entitled 'TSE 300 Composite -- Computation Formulae and Assumptions' was provided by the Bank of Canada.

Reference period and unit of measurement

The source index start date was 1 January 1977, with previous data retrospectively calculated. It is based on 1975 = 1000, reflects end of month figures and starts in January 1956. Weekly calculations were carried out for the period 1971 to 1975, while the index has been compiled daily from 1976 with effectively an instantaneous release.

The MEI series refers to end of month

DATA MANIPULATION

Aggregation method and weights

The index is a market weighted index measuring the current aggregate market value as a proportion of an average base aggregate market value, both relating to float shares as defined above. The former is derived as the sum of the products of presently outstanding shares and current prices, while the latter as the sum of the products of outstanding shares as at 1 January 1975 and trade weighted average 1975 prices.

Changes to the current market value (other than those induced by pure price movements) necessitate adjustments to the base aggregate market value such that there is no impact on the resulting index. The manner in the way these adjustments are made varies with the type of capital change.

Several changes in capital are considered, with the adjustments usually incorporated as they become effective or as soon as the Exchange is informed. They include:

- issuance or withdrawal of stock
- stock rights
- company liquidation
- asset spin-off
- take-over, amalgamation, merger
- bankruptcy
- control block adjustment

For stock dividends in kind; rights distributions; and cash distributions of less than 4% of the underlying stock price based on the last traded board lot, no adjustment is made. Thus, at the open on the ex-date, the stock price of the underlying issue will fall and the index will register a downward change. But where such dividends and distributions are equal to or greater than 4%, an adjustment to the index is made by calculating a value for the distribution and adjusting the last traded board lot price of the stock by that amount. This change causes an adjustment to the base value such that the index level will not be impacted by the price change. The last traded board lot of shares is defined as:

- 1000 shares for securities selling under $0.10
- 500 shares for securities selling over $0.10 and under $1.00
- 100 shares for securities selling at $1.00 and over.

MEXICO

Title in Publication

MSE Share Price Index

CONCEPTS AND COVERAGE

Definition

The Mexican Share Price Index is compiled by the Mexican Stock Exchange (MSE) and is based on price movements in a representative sample of shares quoted daily on the exchange.

Coverage

The index covers the industrial, commercial and service sectors.

The sample is updated every two months to ensure the selection criteria still apply. At present there are 35 companies included, but the sample number has varied between 35 and 50.

The sample is purposive with the selection criteria being primarily based on trading volumes. Companies are ranged by decreasing trading volume, from high through medium to low, with the first two categories being divided into quartiles. All companies are selected down to and including the first quartile of the second category. The sample is then completed with companies from the second quartile of the medium trading volume category. In this case, however, additional criteria on capitalisation values and sector of activity are also employed.

If there are there are two or more share classes for one company and if these classes represent more than 15% of the capitalisation of the sample, only that share class with the higher/highest trading volume will be included in the index calculation.

Excluded from selection are companies whose shares are, or will be, suspended for at least one month. Subsidiaries of a holding company are also excluded if both the subsidiary and the holding company have high trading volumes and the subsidiary represents over 75% of the holding company's assets.

SOURCE

Source Agencies

Data are compiled by the exchange and published by the Bank of Mexico.

Key national publication sources

Bank of Mexico: Carpeta de Indicadores Economicos, Indice de precios de las acciones cotizadas: indice general.

Breakdown available/Other related indices

In addition to the total index, indices are calculated for 6 sectors of economic activity: Mining, Manufacturing, Construction, Trade, Transport and Communication, Services.

Methodological references

A methodological note has been published by the Mexican Stock Exchange entitled 'Indice de precios y cotizaciones , Selection Characteristics and Criteria'.

Reference period and unit of measurement

Monthly indices are calculated by the exchange as the arithmetic average of daily indices. The source indices are available from 1970 on the base of 78 in October 1978.

The MEI series is end of month figures.

DATA MANIPULATION

Aggregation method and weights

Daily indices are calculated as the ratio of the weighted average of price quotations of the current trading day over the corresponding average of the previous trading day. Weights used to calculate the aggregated indices are derived from the market capitalisation value of the current day of each company within the sample capitalisation.

Adjustments to capitalisation values are made to take account of capital increases and decreases resulting from new issues, subscription rights, increase in shares at conversion of convertible bonds, mergers, etc.

UNITED STATES

Title in Publication

NYSE Common Stocks

CONCEPTS AND COVERAGE

Definition

The Composite Index of all common stocks listed on the New York Stock Exchange (NYSE) was established by the exchange in 1966 along with four sub-group indices. These indices are a measure of the changes in aggregate market value of NYSE common stocks. They are adjusted to eliminate the effects of capitalisation changes, new listings and delistings.

Coverage

All common shares are used in the compilations, including those of foreign registered companies and investment funds. In excess of 2200 common stocks are presently listed on the NYSE and thus dominance by one stock is minimal.

SOURCE

Source Agencies

The NYSE compiles and disseminates the indices which are also published in the Federal Reserve Bulletin.

Key national publication source

Federal Reserve Bulletin: Financial Markets 1.36 Stock Market Selected Statistics: Common Stock Prices NYSE.

Breakdown available/Other related indices

Four sub-group indices - Industrial, Transportation, Utility and Finance - are compiled and published. There are numerous other price indices compiled for United States stock trading including Standard and Poor's, the NASDAQ, the American Stock Exchange, the Dow-Jones Industrial Average.

Methodological references

The Common Stock Indexes (1938-1988), Business Research Department, NYSE inc.

Reference period and unit of measurement

The original series is based 31 December 1965 = 50, with the composite index retrospectively compiled to May 1964. A consistent historical record for the composite has been computed from 1939 to 1964 through a conversion of the former Securities Exchange Commission price index to the 1965 base.

The MEI series is the monthly average of daily closing indices.

DATA MANIPULATION

Aggregation method and weights

Quoted closing prices are used for the daily index, although the indices are compiled and electronically disseminated every 15 seconds.

The market value of each stock is obtained by multiplying its price per share by the number of shares listed. The aggregate market value, which is the sum of the individual market values, is then expressed as a relative of the base period market value.

Any change in the capitalisation of an individual issue or of all issues in aggregate is dealt with through a proportionate change in the market value of the base figure. The indices thus reflect only movements resulting from auction market activity.

The aggregated indices are arithmetically weighted according to the market capitalisation of each stock. Calculation is performed in two stages:

a) computation of the current index
b) daily adjustment to the base market values for capitalisation changes

The procedures for adjustments are:

– Stock splits and stock dividends -- no adjustment since the aggregate market value does not change.
– New listings/delistings -- require an increase/decrease in the base market value proportional to the change in the aggregate market value of the list.
– Mergers between two listed companies resulting in no change in total value require no adjustment.
– Mergers an a listed company and an unlisted company require an adjustment for the additional value added.
– In rights offerings an adjustment in the base is made to compensate for the value of the new shares being added to the current value of the issue.

AUSTRALIA

Title in Publication

The ASX All Ordinaries

CONCEPTS AND COVERAGE

Definition

The All Ordinaries Index is Australia's broad market index representing over 90% of the domestic market capitalisation of the Australian Stock Exchange (ASX). It summarizes movements in share values resulting from equity trading on the ASX.

Coverage

All companies, domestic and foreign, listed on the exchange are eligible for inclusion provided they meet the following criteria:

- All securities must have the character of ordinary equity. The index thus normally includes quoted ordinary shares, both fully and partly paid, rights, bonuses, deferred settlement shares (which normally result from new issues or capital reconstructions) and listed trust units. Excluded are options, warrants, convertible notes and preference shares, but a few participating preference and/or convertible preference shares may be included as secondary issues provided they are linked to the main equity issues by a fixed ratio, form a substantial part of the company's capital, are well traded, participate in all pro-rata issues and have no cash alternative to their conversion to equity. Excluded also are shares whose sale is currently prohibited by legislation, ASX regulations, company articles, etc.
- New floats need to demonstrate regular trading patterns of liquidity, turnover, shareholder spread, etc., before they can be considered for inclusion. Exceptions would relate to large floats such as the privatisation of a large state enterprise.
- A company must achieve minimum standards of index market capitalisation and liquidity.

No adjustments are made for control blocks, cross share holdings or other long term holdings unless there are legal contracts preventing the sale of shares therein.

Since the number of companies in the index is not fixed, securities removed are not necessarily immediately replaced. Removals can result from an inadequate market capitalisation, low liquidity, absorbtion in mergers, etc.

% Weighting and Number of Components

	December 1990	December 1995
Number of Companies	242	320
	%	%
Gold and Other Metals	19.12	17.89
Diversified Resources	12.83	13.04
Banking and Finance	9.93	15.61
Diversified Industrials	12.92	3.90
Media	1.61	9.50
Other	43.59	40.06
Total	100.00	100.00

SOURCE

Source agencies

The All Ordinaries Index is calculated and maintained by the ASX.

Key national publication source:

The Reserve Bank of Australia Bulletin, F5, Share Markets, All Ordinaries.

Breakdown available/Other related indices

The index is divided into All Industrials (70% of the total) and All Resources (30%). These are further broken into 24 industry sector indices. Allocation to a sector is determined by an analysis of the company's present and future sources of profit, asset allocation and revenue.

The exchange also produces Total Return Indices showing pre-tax returns after total re-investment of dividends.

Methodological references

'Companies on the Australian Stock Exchange Indices', published every six months by ASX Index Services, describes the compilations involved. Further information is available from this source.

Reference period and unit of measurement

The source index, introduced in January 1980, is calculated and disseminated daily. The monthly index, based on 31 December 1979 = 500, is an average of daily figures. Sydney and Melbourne indices were calculated from 1958 and 1960 respectively, while earlier retrospective calculations record monthly market movements back to 1875.

The MEI series is the monthly average of daily figures.

DATA MANIPULATION

Aggregation method and weights

The Index Market Capitalisation of each company is determined by multiplying the number of quoted shares (or units) by their market price and their respective Weighting Factor (usually 100%). This factor reflects market availability of shares and/or low liquidity. The price used is the last recorded sale price, modified by any subsequent higher bid or lower offer made before closing. If no trading takes place on a given day, the previous last sale price is used.

Company market capitalisation figures are added together and the index calculated as follows:

$$\text{Today's index} =$$

$$\text{Yesterday's index} * \frac{\text{Today's closing index market capitalisation}}{\text{Today's start of day index market capitalisation}}$$

The start of day index market capitalisation value is the previous day's closing index market capitalisation figure adjusted for any overnight changes to the index portfolio, such as delistings, additions new issues and capital reconstructions. These overnight adjustments to the number of shares and prices do not move the indices, which are designed solely to reflect movements resulting from share trading during regular trading hours.

Because of the method of calculation, the index is chain-linked and weighted by market capitalisation.

JAPAN

Title in Publication

TSE TOPIX

CONCEPTS AND COVERAGE

Definition

The Tokyo Stock Exchange (TSE) TOPIX is a composite price index of all common stocks listed on the First Section of the Tokyo exchange.

Coverage

The exchange is divided into two sections, the first of which is in effect the market for the stocks of larger companies (presently numbering some 1300), while the second is for those of smaller and newly-listed companies. For a stock to be included in the first section it must meet criteria regarding payment of dividends, trading volumes, number of listed shares, the degree of control by major shareholders and the dispersion of the shares among shareholders.

Excluded are foreign companies, subsidiaries of foreign companies and investment funds.

Included are the common stocks of companies with significant levels of public ownership if such common stocks qualify for listing in the First Section.

Given the large number of stocks in the computation, dominance by one stock is minimised.

SOURCE

Source Agencies

The index is computed and published by the Tokyo Stock Exchange.

Key national publication sources

Data are published in the Monthly Statistics Report, Banking and Finance, Stock Prices, Tokyo stock price indices, Total average.

Breakdown available/Other related indices

Indices for 33 subgroups are compiled, as are three indices by size classification (companies with 200 million or more shares, those with 60 million or more but under 200 million, those with fewer than 60 million).

Methodological references

A detailed note describing the characteristics and manner of computation of the TOPIX was made available.

Reference period and unit of measurement

The TOPIX and the sub-indices are compiled and disseminated each minute. Although the TOPIX was introduced in 1969, it is available on a daily closing basis from 1949, the sub-indices from the original base date of 4 January 1968. Certain additional sub-indices introduced in 1993, however, are available only from 4 January 1983. The TOPIX is based on 4 January 1968 = 100.

The monthly index is the average of daily closing data and is the one shown in the MEI.

DATA MANIPULATION

Aggregation method and weights

The TOPIX is weighted by market capitalisation in that it is derived as the relationship of the current aggregate market value (the sum of the market values of all individual stocks, each obtained through multiplying the number of listed shares by the current price) to the comparable aggregate market value of the base period.

The priority of prices used in the compilation is given in the following order:

1) a specially devised 'quote' price aimed at negating bids and offers exceeding a reasonable range of variation;

2) a traded price observed at time of computation;
3) in the absence of quote or traded price, the following (in the order given):
   a. a theoretical price applied to ex-rights situations
   b. the latest quote price
   c. the latest traded price

No adjustment is made in respect to share price changes due to dividend payments.

With respect to corporate decisions, no adjustment is made in cases where the decision entails no change in the market value of the share, i.e. stock split-up, stock split-down and decrease in paid-in capital, since the new stock price multiplied by the increased (decreased) number of shares is theoretically the same as the old stock price multiplied by the old number of shares. Adjustments are made to the base market value in respect of new listings; delistings; rights offerings to shareholders; public offerings; private placements; mergers; exercise of stock subscription warrants; conversion of convertible bonds or convertible preferred stock into common stock; purchase and retirement of company's own stock.

KOREA

Title in Publication

KSE KOSPI

CONCEPTS AND COVERAGE

Definition

The Korea Composite Stock Price Index (KOSPI) of the Korea Stock Exchange (KSE) measures changes in the selling prices of all shares listed on the exchange.

Coverage

The KSE has two sections to which companies are assigned according to criteria relating financial history, share distribution and trading volume. The index construction includes all shares quoted on each section. It includes both common stock and preferred stock, although the latter are securities that are closely related to common stock, with a dividend rate set at a 1% above that of common stock.

SOURCE

Source Agencies

The exchange compiles and publishes the daily index.

Key national statistical sources

Monthly data are provided in the Monthly Statistical Bulletin of the Bank of Korea.

Breakdown available/ Other related series

Supplemental indices have been developed: by section (2), by industry (34) and by capital size (3).

Reference period and unit of measurement

The daily source series is compiled on the base of 4th April 1980 = 100 and is available from January 1975. Monthly data are compiled both for end of period values and as averages of daily indices.

The MEI series relates to averages of daily indices.

DATA MANIPULATION

Aggregation method and weights

The index is a weighted market value index where weights, based on companies' capitalisations, are constantly adjusted. The base market value is adjusted whenever the current market value undergoes variations not associated with market trading, i.e. it is adjusted to take account of capital issues, new listings, delistings, mergers and acquisitions, etc. The basic principle for adjusment is to make the index on the last trading day before the effective date of the corporate action equal to the index on the effective date. Newly listed shares are, however, not incorporated into the index until the 31st. trading day after listing.

Since January 1983, the index has been compiled according the the Paasche formula.

Common stock prices are applied to both common stock and preferred stock. (The prices of preferred stock show the same trend as those of common stock). The prices used in the compilation are daily selling quotations at closing. If no transactions take place for a given day, the previous day's quotation is used.

NEW ZEALAND

Title in Publication

NZSE Capital Index

CONCEPTS AND COVERAGE

Definition

The New Zealand Stock Exchange (NZSE) Capital Index is one of two major and complementary indices produced by the exchange, the other being the Gross Index, a return index calculated on the basis of all dividends being re-invested. Both were developed to provide a comprehensive measurement of price trends of New Zealand listed issuers on the NZSE.

Coverage

The Capital Index relates to the equity securities of all listed companies, approximating some 150 in total. Equity securites are generally those carrying a right to vote or to participate in the assets of the company, or those which may be converted into securities having such voting or participation rights.

Fixed interest securities and overseas listed issuers are excluded.

In mid-1996, 5 companies accounted for more than 50% of the all ordinaries capitalisation. One company, Telecom, represented almost 25%.

SOURCE

Source Agencies

The NZSE compiles and publishes the data. The index is forwarded to the OECD by the Reserve Bank of New Zealand.

Key national publication sources

Data are not published in National Statistical issues but indices are included in most official NZSE publications.

Breakdown available/Other related indices

Both the Capital and Gross indices are sub-divided into 25 market sectors. Additionally, the NZSE produces, amongst others, the NZSE10, NZSE30 and NZSE40 indices (on both a Capital and Gross basis) and the Smaller Companies Index.

Methodological references

A methodological note by the NZSE on the theory and construction of the indices was provided.

Reference period and unit of measurement

The Capital Index starts in January 1967 and is based on 1 July 1968 = 1000.

The monthly index, and the MEI index, are averages of daily figures.

DATA MANIPULATION

Aggregation method and weights

The Capital Index is not adjusted for dividends, thus reflecting the fall in share price when the security is quoted ex-dividend.

The previous end-of-day index is updated with the ratio of the market capitalisation at the end of the current day over the adjusted current day opening market capitalisation, such adjustments reflecting changes in capital. The market value of a security is taken to be the latest market price multiplied by the number of shares.

AUSTRIA

Title in Publication

VSE WBI Index

CONCEPTS AND COVERAGE

Definition

The Vienna Stock Exchange WBI (Wiener Borse Index) share index relates to all Official Market shares quoted on the spot market and thus reflects movements on the Austrian stock market as a whole.

Coverage

The Official Market is the largest and most important segment of the exchange dealing with securities of high trading volumes, warrants and almost all bonds. The remaining two segments, the Semi-Official and the Unregulated, are concerned with newly traded companies, companies with a restricted number of free shares, etc. Criteria for admission to the Official Market relate to a specified minimum nominal value of the company's shares, to a three year financial history of the company, to a lack of any buying restrictions on trading in the company's shares, to the number of 'free' shares available for trading, etc.

Foreign registered companies and investment funds are not included.

There are over 100 stocks now being traded on the Official Market.

SOURCE

Source Agencies

The index is computed and published by the Vienna Stock Exchange.

Key national publication sources

Data can be obtained from:

- The Vienna Stock Exchange -- daily Official Price List, Monthly Statistical Report, Annual Report and via electronic means;
- Oesterreichische Nationalbank--Statistisches Monatsheft: Kapitalmarkt, Oesterreichische Aktienmarkt;
- WIFO -- Statistische Ubersichten, 2-Einlagen, Kredite, Geldvolumen, Kapitalmarkt;
- (This last is the MEI source).

Breakdown available/Other related series

Sub indices relating to 12 sectors are published, covering banks, insurance, construction, building materials, breweries, chemicals, energy, machines/transport/technology, foods, pulp/paper, trade/services, real estate.

% Weighting and Number of Components

2 January 1991		28 December 1995	
No.	%	No.	%
1	10.39	1	7.94
2	9.15	2	7.84
3	9.12	3	7.53
4	6.65	4	7.49
5	6.53	5	6.45
6	5.59	6	4.64
7	3.35	7	4.42
8-85	49.22	8-113	53.69
	100.00		100.00

Additional indices such as the WBI 30 and the Austrian Traded Index are also published.

Methodological references

A description is available on the Internet from the exchange entitled 'Vienna Stock Exchange, General Information, Organisation of the Exchange, the Vienna Stock Exchange Share indices' (http://www.vienna-stock-exchange.at/boerse).

Reference period and unit of measurement

The index is available daily on the Internet and in the Official Price List, monthly in the publications noted above. The index is based on 31 December 1967 = 100. The monthly figures in the MEI relate to the 15th of the month, while those in the national publications are end of month.

DATA MANIPULATION

Aggregation method and weights

The index is an arithmetic mean weighted according to the market capitalisation of the company and calculated at closing according to the Paasche fomula.

For shares traded in consecutive days, closing price is used. For shares for which only one price is fixed per trading session, the day's price is used. If no price or estimated price has been derived during a trading session, the last available price or estimated price is used. No adjustment is made in respect of share price changes due to dividend payments.

Adjustments are made in cases of changes in the capital of a company (capital increases or reductions) and when new shares are admitted to listing.

BELGIUM

Title in Publication

The BSE Belgian All Shares

CONCEPTS AND COVERAGE

Definition

The BSE (Brussels Stock Exchange) Belgian All Shares Index covers all Belgian shares quoted on the exchange's First Market, which deals with both spot and forward transactions. Prior to June 1996, the index related only to spot transactions, whereas from this date some Belgian shares are quoted on the forward market. However, the company composition of the index has not changed.

Coverage

Excluded from index calculations are units in investment funds and foreign registered companies. New shares are included as soon as they are introduced on to the exchange. Similarly, suppressed shares are excluded from the index on the day of delisting.

Key national publication sources

The daily index is also published in the press and via data vendors.

The monthly average is compiled by the Bank and published in the Bulletin de la Banque Nationale de Belgique: 9-Activité boursière, Valeurs belges, cours des actions - dividendes non-réinvestis.

The daily and monthly indices are also available in the Bank's database 'Belgostat' (Marché boursier - Belgian All Share - indice des cours).

Methodological references

A descriptive note, 'Les indices de la Bourse de Bruxelles', was provided to the OECD.

% Weighting and Number of Components

	September 1994		December 1996	
	%	No.	%	No.
Banking and Finance	12.05	18	16.05	10
Chemicals	8.70	17	10.95	17
Oil	8.79	3	6.26	3
Electricals	18.43	6	19.27	4
Insurance	6.40	6	8.34	3
Holdings	23.47	90	20.21	63
Other	22.16	248*	18.91	80
Total	100.00	388	100.00	180

* including small caps

SOURCE

Source Agencies

The Brussels Stock Exchange both compiles and publishes the index (in its monthly report 'Indices and Statistics').

Reference period and unit of measurement

The daily and end of month indices of the exchange are closing indices and are based on 1 January 1980 = 1000 with release starting in January 1985.

End of month figures have also been calculated for 1980 to 1984.

The MEI series, calculated and supplied by the Bank, is an average of daily figures.

DATA MANIPULATION

Aggregation and weights

The index is compiled using a Paasche formula. It is an arithmetic mean weighted according to the market capitalisation of the company. The daily value of the index is computed at closing by dividing the stock capitalisation of all quotations included in the index by a base amount. The resulting ratio is then multiplied by the starting value of the index.

The base amount is adjusted to keep the index consistent. After the market close on the eve of an action involving a change in capitalisation of a type detailed below, and before the next opening of the market, an adjustment to the base is effected:

- Introduction of a new company or a new category of securities; delisting of a company or category of securities -- the stock capitalisation base is modified in the same proportion that the increase (or decrease) in stock has in relation to the capitalisation of the previous day's index.
- Increase or decrease in the number of existing securities -- the stock capitalisation base is modified to take account of the changed number of shares and their previous day quotation.
- Transactions relating to mergers are treated as delisting of companies and an incorporation of the new company or, if the merger results from the absorption of a company, as an increase of capitalisation with or without delisting depending on whether the company was previously included in the index.

Requiring no adjustment are transactions including bonus issues, stock splits (up or down), take overs,etc.

No adjustment is made in respect of share price changes due to dividend payments.

CZECH REPUBLIC

Title in Publication

The CNB-120

CONCEPTS AND COVERAGE

Definition

The Czech National Bank CNB-120 monitors trends in the share price movements of 120 issues traded on the Prague Stock Exchange. The component companies are chosen to reflect the economy as a whole and thus all industries, except those classified as 'Other', are represented.

Coverage

For the purposes of the index, an industrial classification of some 25 sectors is employed with the intent that there are no fewer than 4 component companies in each sector. The main criteria for the selection of components relate to the liquidity of the share, where cumulative trading must exceed a specified value amount, to the number of shares issued and to satisfactory trading stability. In principle investment funds are included if four eligible representatives are available. A review of the index components is conducted yearly.

SOURCE

Source Agencies

The Czech National Bank compiles and disseminates the index.

Breakdown available/Other related series

Also compiled are the CNB-Global covering all shares traded on the exchange; the 1st Wave index relating to the first companies privatised; the 2nd Wave index relating to those companies privatised at a later date; and, for all the general indices noted above, industrial sector indices.

Reference period and unit of measurement

The present index is based on 1 March 1995 = 1000. A previous index with a base of 16 December 1993 = 1000 was produced but with no linking to the present version. As a consequence no figures for the present index exist prior to its base date.

The MEI series is the average of daily figures.

DATA MANIPULATION

Aggregation methods and weights

Individual price indices are developed for each of the 120 components. The summation is a weighted geometric average of the latest daily transaction price changes, weighted by market capitalisation as it applied in a recent year. Prices are adjusted to eliminate the price variation associated with dividend payments.

DENMARK

Title in Publication

CSE All Shares Index

CONCEPTS AND COVERAGE

Definition

The Copenhagen Stock Exchange (CSE) All Shares Index is designed to show price movements of all Danish shares quoted on the exchange.

Coverage

All Danish shares quoted on the primary and secondary markets (sections 1 and 2) of the exchange are used in the calculation of the index, with the exception of foreign registered companies, investment funds and two large holding companies. Some 200 companies are presently listed.

SOURCE

Source Agencies

The Copenhagen Stock Exchange compiles the index which is published by Danmarks Statistik.

Key national publication sources

The series published in MEI is available in Danmarks Statistik's 'Statistik manedsoversigt', table 45.

Breakdown available/Other related series

Also published is a sub-index relating to industrial shares. Other separate indices relating to Banks, Trade and shipping and Insurance are computed but not currently published.

Methodological references

Descriptions are given in 'Statistiske Efterretinger, Penge- og Kapitalmarked, No 3, 1983'.

Reference period and unit of measurement

The index started in 1983 and is based on 3 January 1983 = 100. Monthly data refer to end of month.

The MEI series also relate to end of month.

DATA MANIPULATION

Aggregation method and weights

The index is a weighted market value index where the original weights based on the companies' nominal capital value on 3 January 1983 are constantly adjusted to take account of capital changes and share price changes associated with dividend payments. It is compiled as a Laspeyres index using the market capitalisation of the company as weights for price changes. Calculations use the quoted bid price.

Adjustments to share prices are made to eliminate changes due to dividend payments by a increasing reduction of the ex-dividend price of a share. This reduction is increased daily by 1/360 of the amount of the dividend.

Adjustments to capital values are made when there are new issues, when companies enter or leave the exchange. No adjustment is made for stock dividends.

FINLAND

Title in Publication

The HEX All Share Index

CONCEPTS AND COVERAGE

Definition

The HEX (Helsinki Stock Exchange) price and yield series of indices include the All Share price index, which represents trends in share prices exclusive of dividend re-investment.

Coverage

The All Share index is a non-weight-restricted index calculated from all shares listed on the Official List of the exchange and thus does not reflect share series listed on the OTC list and the Brokers' list. At present, 76 companies are admitted to the Official list, covering all sectors of the economy. Indices at the sector level are produced, with the classification of a company to a sector being determined by net sales data. If more than 60% of net sales are produced in one sector, classification is to that sector. If the company does not derive 50% from a single sector, the classification is to 'multi-business'. For the remaining cases, classification is determined by the company and the exchange in consultation. Investment funds are excluded from the index calculation, but foreign companies are not. Only publicly accessible shares are considered.

SOURCE

Source Agency

The source agency is the Helsinki Stock Exchange.

Key national publication sources

The All Share index and certain sector indices are published by the Bank of Finland in its Monthly Bulletin.

Breakdown available/ Other related series

Share specific price indices are compiled. Price and yield indices are compiled at the all share level, at the 16 sector level and at the HEX 20 level, this last index relating to the top 20 share series with the highest turnover. In addition, the HEX portfolio index, both price and yield versions, is constructed where the weight accorded to any single company cannot exceed 10%.

Methodological references

A descriptive booklet produced by the exchange, entitled 'HEX INDEX', was provided.

% Weighting and Number of Components

	1990		1996	
	%	No.	%	No.
Banks and Finance	15.60	8	4.70	5
Insurance and Invstment	12.00	16	3.90	7
Other Services	13.50	15	9.80	15
Metal Industry	12.50	7	15.10	11
Forest Industry	16.90	5	14.70	5
Multi-Business Industry	21.00	12	4.30	7
Other Industries	8.50	14	47.50	22
Total	100.00	77	100.00	72
of which, top company is	6.60		28.00	

Reference period and unit of measurement

Daily closing indices are calculated after free trading is finished. Periodic indices are calculated at the close of each period as the arithmetic mean of closing indices for each trading day in the period in question.

All HEX indices are based on 28 December 1990 = 1000 and have been calculated retroactively to the beginning of 1987.

The MEI series is the average of daily closing figures.

DATA MANIPULATION

Aggregation method and weights

The calculation of the HEX All Share index is based on the Paasche formula and measures changes in the market capitalisation of the shares caused by changes in share prices. It is intended to eliminate index fluctuations and inconsistencies in share volumes and prices caused by events not connected to the operation of the market. The index is defined as a arithmetic mean, weighted according to the market capitalisation of the company at current value.

Daily price alterations are chained into indices, with the closing index of the previous trading day used as a base number for the trading day's computations.

The price used is the last transaction price of the day. If no price is available, a substitute price is evaluated. An individual bid, offer or previous trading price can be selected depending on the existing prices at the time of calculation and the value of the previous trading price in relation to that of the bids and offers.

Events requiring adjustments include:

- a new share issue
- splitting of shares
- increase or decrease in the number of shares
- mergers
- bonus issues
- delisting of a company
- suspension of trading

FRANCE

Title in Publication

Bourse de Paris SBF 250

CONCEPTS AND COVERAGE

Definition

The SBF 250 index is compiled from a sample of approximately 250 companies selected from all French equities listed on the First and Second sections of the Bourse.

Coverage

The index is compiled as a total index and for 12 sectors (and 18 sub-sectors), which are aggregated into 3 groups, namely Industrials, Services and Financials. Selection is based on the sample's representativeness of the total capitalisation of each of the 12 economic sectors and on the regularity of trading. Stocks are ranked, in sector and in descending order, by capitalisation. Those with the highest capitalisation and which are traded on more than 70% of all trading days are chosen, with the intent that each sample represents an identical percentage, currently over 90%, of its sector's market capitalisation. The review of the constituent stocks is carried out once a year. However, at the end of each quarter, stocks which have been de-listed, have been subject to mergers or have traded on fewer than 50% of the trading days in the previous 12 months are replaced.

Units in investment funds are excluded. Shares of foreign companies listed on the Bourse may be included provided that the issuer's central decision - making body is in France and that the Bourse accounts for a representative portion of total trading in the stock.

% Weighting and Number of Components

	1993 %	1996 %
Industrial Values	**49.14**	**54.54**
Energy	7.60	8.67
Primary Goods	4.35	6.03
Construction	6.42	5.10
Investment Goods	9.70	7.42
Cars	3.52	4.63
Other Consumer Goods	9.64	13.42
Agriculture/Food Industry	7.91	9.28
Services	**18.26**	**23.32**
Distribution	7.32	11.25
Other Services	10.94	12.08
Financial Companies	**32.60**	**22.13**
Real Estate	3.57	2.00
Financial Services	22.24	14.58
Investment Companies	6.79	5.56
Total	100.00	100.00

SOURCE

Source agencies

The Bourse compiles the index, which is published both by the Bourse and the Institut National de la Statistique et des Études Économiques (INSEE).

Key national publication sources

The series is available in INSEE's Bulletin Mensuel de Statistique, tableau 35, Indicateurs boursiers, Indice SBF 250 and in the Bourse's Revue Mensuelle Actions.

Breakdown available/Other related indices

Group, sector and sub-sector indices as noted above are produced, as price and return indices. The SBF 120 and other indices are also produced.

Methodological references

Various descriptive details are to be found in the Bourse publication 'The Paris Bourse Indices -- Methodology and Review'.

Reference period and unit of measurement

Figures published by the Bourse relate to monthly closing indices. The series, based on 28 December 1990 = 1000, starts in January 1991.

The MEI series is the INSEE series which is averages of daily closing figures.

DATA MANIPULATION

Aggregation method and weights

The index is compiled using the Laspeyres formula as a ratio of the capitalisation of issues in the sample over the capitalisation of the sample in the base year. This base value is adjusted to reflect capital changes in the existing sample stock, de-listings, new listings, etc. Prices used in the calculations are the prices of actual trades, the previous price when no trading has taken place or estimates in the case of public offerings, buy-outs and swap offers.

GERMANY

Title in Publication

CDAX Share Price Index

CONCEPTS AND COVERAGE

Definition

The CDAX Share Price Index (prior to 1 January 1996 known as the FWBX index) includes all ordinary and preferred shares of all German based companies listed on the Frankfurt Stock Exchange.

Coverage

The index covers some 300 companies and 350 issues. There are no restrictions on the entry of companies to official listing and thus the index can include those companies with significant levels of state ownership. The compilation, however, is restricted to shares deemed to be deliverable. Shares newly introduced are included in the index calculation immediately after listing. Similarly there is an immediate elimination of shares that are withdrawn.

SOURCE

Source agencies

The source index is compiled by the Deutsche Boerse A G, Frankfurt am Main.

Key national publication sources

The index is published by the Deutsche Bundesbank in its Monthly Report, VII Capital Market, 5 Yields and Indices on Domestic Securities, CDAX share price index and in the Statistical Supplement to the Monthly Report, 2 Capital market statistics. This published series relates to end of month.

Breakdown available/Other related indices

16 sub-indices are computed for industrial sectors, ten of which are published by the Deutsche Bundesbank. The Composite DAX index is a performance index matching the CDAX share price index. Several other indices are also published, including the DAX, a performance index relating to a portfolio of 30 standard shares and the related DAX Share Price index.

Methodological references

Descriptive information is included in Deutsche Bundesbank Capital Market Statistics, 1997. Additionally, a methodological note entitled 'Composite DAX, CDAX, Deutsche Boerse' was provided to the OECD.

Reference period and unit of measurement

The CDAX share price index is end of month, based on 30 December 1987 = 100, and has been retroactively linked to the time series of the FWB index of the Frankfurt Stock Exchange starting in 1970. The MEI series is an average of closing daily figures and starts in 1974.

DATA MANIPULATION

Aggregation method and weights

The CDAX share price index is capital weighted Laspeyres index, where the price of each share is weighted according to the number of shares listed and declared deliverable. The weights are adjusted using correction factors which are set to 1.0 once a year. This annual updating of the weighting factors to a level of 1.0 would result in a break in the index; this is avoided through the use of a chain index factor in the calculation formula. Price distortions which arise in the case of capital changes (capital increases with subscription rights, capital adjustments, issue of bonus shares, reductions of capital, admissions and retirements of public limited companies) are eliminated through adjustment factors which are applied at the level of the individual stock. Price variations associated with dividend payments are not eliminated.

The last actual quoted price, i.e. the price at which the share has been traded on the market, is the basis for the computation of the CDAX share price index.

GREECE

Title in Publication

ASE Composite

CONCEPTS AND COVERAGE

Definition

The Athens Stock Exchange (ASE) Composite index is a stock capitalisation weighted index, calculated on the basis of all types of shares selected for inclusion in the index.

Coverage

Shares are ranked according to criteria which take account of market capitalisation and turnover. 75 shares are presently included, accounting for nearly 75% of total market capitalisation. No foreign companies are listed on the exchange. Investment and holding companies are included but currently represent approximately 5% of the sample's weight. The weight accorded to the OTE telecommunications company is restricted to 12.9%, significantly below its actual weighting.

SOURCE

Source agencies

The ASE compiles and publishes the index, which is transmitted to the OECD by the Bank of Greece.

Breakdown available/Other related series

A breakout of the total index into 9 sub-indices is also published by the source.

Methodological references

The Annual Statistical Bulletin of the Athens Stock Exchange.

Reference period and unit of measurement

The index is computed and published daily, monthly and annually.

The ASE series are based on 31 December 1980 = 100, except the Leasing sub-index which is 31 December 1987 = 100.

The MEI series is the monthly index , an average of the daily indices, which relate to closing figures.

% Weighting and Number of Components

	1995	
	%	No.
Banks	38	10
Leasing	2	2
Insurance	1	3
Investment	2	5
Industrial	39	28
Construction	11	14
Holdings	3	6
Miscellaneous	4	7
Total	100.00	75

DATA MANIPULATION

Aggregation method and weights

The index is computed as the arithmetic weighted average of the sample shares, using share capitalisation within the sample's total capitalisation as weight. The index is derived as a ratio of current capitalisation over base year capitalisation. Changes in capitalisation not associated with price movements in the market are taken into account through a daily adjustment of the denominator.

Prices used are those at closing, with no adjustment made for variations due to dividend payment.

ICELAND

Title in Publication

The ISE Share Price Index

CONCEPTS AND COVERAGE

Definition

The ISE (Iceland Stock Exchange) Share Price Index reflects price movements of shares traded on the exchange.

Coverage

The index covers all companies quoted on the exchange.

Reference period and unit of measurement

The index is based on 1 January 1993 = 1000. No data are available prior to this date. Daily and monthly series are calculated, the latter as averages of the daily indices.

The MEI series is an average of daily indices.

DATA MANIPULATION

Aggregation method and weights

The index is derived as the current level of share prices relative to the level which prevailed on the base date. It is calculated daily from the latest quoted prices and is based on weights which are derived from the market value of each company's share capital. The formula is based on the chained Paasche method.

IRELAND

Title in Publication

The ISEQ Overall

CONCEPTS AND COVERAGE

Definition

The ISEQ (Irish Stock Exchange Equity Index) series, of which the Overall is a component, has been devised and is compiled by the Irish Stock Exchange. The Overall measures the change in the prices of ordinary stocks and shares quoted on the exchange.

Coverage

The ISEQ Overall relates to Republic of Ireland and Northern Ireland companies quoted on the Official List of the exchange and thus excludes companies listed on the DCM (Developing Companies Market) and the ESM (Exploration Securities Market) sections of the exchange. The capitalisation of these other sections is small in comparison with that of the Official List. The index excludes units in investment funds. Some 80 companies are covered in the compilation.

SOURCE

Source Agency

The Irish Stock Exchange is the producing agency.

Key national publication sources

The exchange publishes a Monthly Bulletin containing month and year-to-date data for the full range of the ISEQ series. This bulletin also provides information on market turnover, ISEQ weightings, sensitivity indicators showing how much a move in the price of a stock has moved the overall index, dividend payments, etc.

The index series is reproduced through electronic news services, by the press and in the Central Statistical Office's Bulletin, Economic series 7, table 7.25.

Breakdown available/Other related series

The ISEQ series comprises the Overall and two sub-indices, the ISEQ Financial and the ISEQ General. Additionally, the exchange produces return indices in the same structure as the price indices, with the same component companies.

Methodological references

A descriptive note, 'The Irish Stock Exchange Equity Index', was provided by the exchange.

Reference period and unit of measurement

The indices have 1000 on 4 January 1988 as their base and historical data for the Overall has been calculated to the beginning of 1983. The source series relates to closing and is weekly from January 1983 and daily since 1986.

From 1987, the MEI series are values at closing of official business on the first working day of each month; prior to this point they relate to the first Wednesday of each month.

DATA MANIPULATION

Aggregation method and weights.

The index is compiled as a stock capitalisation weighted average. The base value is re-calculated whenever a constituent's issued share capital changes or a new company enters the list. For the purposes of calculating market capitalisation, partly paid shares are adjusted to the fully paid price.

ITALY

Title in Publication

The ISE MIB Storico

CONCEPTS AND COVERAGE

Definition

The MIB (Mercato Italiano di Borsa) Storico of the Italian Stock Exchange (ISE) reflects all stock trading activity on the exchange. The exchange came into being with the 1996 computer integration of the 10 regional exchanges of Italy.

Coverage

All share types of some 220 companies are included in the calculation of the total index. Foreign companies are included. An annual review of the companies admitted to the exchange is conducted to determine if admission criteria are being met. New companies are normally admitted at this time. A comprehensive computation of the index is also performed with this annual review.

Key national publication sources

Daily indices are shown in the economic press, with monthly indices published in the monthly report of the exchange (end of period) and in ISCO Congiuntura Italiano, Rassegna Mensile.

Methodological references

The methodology of the Italian share price indices is described in a note prepared by the Consiglio di Borsa entitled 'Gli Indici dei Corsi Azionari della Borsa Valori Italiana, Maggio 1996'.

Reference period and unit of measurement

The source index is based on 2 January 1975 = 1000 and starts at this point.

The MEI index, computed and supplied by the Bank of Italy, is a monthly average of daily data.

% Weighting and Number of Components

	1990		1995	
	%	No.	%	No.
Industrial Sector	29.57		33.43	
Service Sector	16.08		24.74	
Financial Sector of which:	54.36		41.83	
- Banks	22.42		20.18	
- Insurance	15.93		16.57	
- Other	16.01		5.08	
Total	100.00	229	100.00	221

SOURCE

Source Agencies

The Consiglio di Borsa (the Italian Stock Exchange Council) is the authority for the index and provides information to its agency Ced Borsa which is responsible for the compilation and dissemination of the index output.

DATA MANIPULATION

Aggregation method and weights

The Laypeyres type index is a capitalisation weighted average of elementary indices of each company included in the computation. The price used for an individual stock is the arithmetic mean of closing prices during the trading session for differing blocks of the stock, weighted by the number of issues exchanged. Increases and decreases of capital are incorporated into the compilation by adjusting the base value with a coefficient computed as the ratio of the new and old series, using the same prices. In the case of new company issues, the initial price is deemed to be the closing price of the first day of trading.

NETHERLANDS

Title in Publication

The CBS All Shares Index

CONCEPTS AND COVERAGE

Definition

The Central Bureau of Statistics (CBS) All Share Index is developed from a 'portfolio' of shares. It is obtained from the ratio of the current value of the portfolio to the corresponding value at the base.

Coverage

The portfolio comprises the ordinary shares of every Dutch company admitted to the Official Market of the Amsterdam Stock Exchange. Preference or priority shares are excluded, as are units of investment funds and shares of foreign companies and holding companies. Total shareholder equity is considered with no adjustment being made for blocks of shares held by a single individual or a group of individuals.

SOURCE

Source Agencies

The Central Bureau of Statistics compiles and publishes the index.

Key national publication sources

The data are available in the CBS's a) Statistical Bulletin and b) Financial Statistics.

Breakdown available/Other related indices

Produced also are sub-indices related to Internationals and Domestics, with the latter further sub-divided into financial and non-financial. Additionally, a price index exclusive of Royal Dutch shares is compiled in order to show trends uninfluenced by the significant weight of the shares of this company.

A series of return indices, with dividends assumed to be re-invested, is also available.

Methodological references

The CBS provided descriptive details on the compilation methods employed.

% Weighting and Number of Components

	1990		1995	
	%	No.	%	No.
Mining and extraction	36.5		27.4	2
Consumer goods industries	18.9		14.4	22
Capital goods industries	5.7		6.6	24
Basic industries	6.8		6.2	23
Construction and building	1.0		0.8	12
Transport and communication	2.2		8.1	8
Non-financial services	8.9		12.1	22
Trade	4.7		4.6	34
Banking and Finance	7.2		6.2	11
Insurance	8.2		13.6	4
Total	100.0	145	100.0	162

Reference period and unit of measurement

The source index is based on December 1983 = 100 and starts in December 1952. Daily series at closing are available from January 1980, end of month series for the prior period.

The MEI series is an average of daily figures.

DATA MANIPULATION

Aggregation method and weights

For the calculation of capitalisation values in the portfolio, the number of units allocated to each share is such that the share's capitalisation as a percentage of the portfolio's capitalisation corresponds to the share's total capitalisation as a percentage of total market capitalisation.

Changes in capital structure necessitate a change in the structure of the portfolio. This method of adjustment compares to a revision of base capitalisation used in most other indices. In effect, this process can be viewed as the selling of the portfolio and the simultaneous re-investing of the proceeds in a new portfolio.

Closing prices are used with the last 'bid' or 'ask' if no closing transaction price is available.

No adjustment is made to eliminate price variations associated with dividend payments.

NORWAY

Title in Publication

OSE All Share Index

CONCEPTS AND COVERAGE

Definition

The Olso Stock Exchange (OSE) All Share Index is a capital weighted price index intended to provide a general overview of movements in Norwegian listed shares.

Coverage

Shares of foreign registered companies are excluded. All share classes for all Norwegian registered companies listed on the Main List are included in the compilation. However, for companies in which the state has long-term holdings, only that portion of a company's value that is deemed to be freely transferable is considered. Norsk Hydro, for example, the largest company listed on the exchange, is deemed to have 50% of its share capital freely marketable.

Breakdown available/Other related indices

Four sector indices of the All Share Index are compiled -- Banks, Insurance, Shipping and Industry. Additionally, the OBX index relating to the 25 most traded share classes is also compiled. Review of shares to be included in this index is conducted twice yearly. In contrast to the All Share Index and its sector indices, no adjustment is made to eliminate price falls at 'ex-dividend' dates.

Further indices are calculated on behalf of newspapers.

Methodological references

A note entitled 'Oslo Stock Exchange -- Share Indices' was made available by the Bank of Norway.

% Weighting and Number of Components

	1990		1995	
	%	No.	%	No.
Banks	5.1	12	9.4	8
Insurance	2.9	4	5.0	4
Industry	69.5	71	64.8	70
Shipping	18.1	39	13.5	44
Other	4.4	21	7.3	51
Total	100.00	147	100.00	177

SOURCE

Source Agencies

The Oslo Stock Exchange is responsible for the calculation design, monitoring and control of the indices. A wholly owned subsidiary is responsible for updating the databases and for the production and maintenance of index selections and weightings.

The Bank of Norway transmits the index to the OECD.

Reference period and unit of measurement

The All Share Index and its sector indices are based 1 January 1983 = 100. Prior to Spring 1988, the indices were calculated daily on the basis of closing prices. From that point, they have been calculated every minute during the trading day.

The MEI series relates to closing on the 15th of each month.

DATA MANIPULATION

Aggregation method and weights

The index is market weighted. The market value of a company (or share class) is the latest share price multiplied by the total shares in the company (or share class). Thus the market value of the company (or share class) divided by the aggregate market value corresponds to the company (or share class) weighting.

The index is calculated in accordance with the formula:

$$I(1) = I(0)*[M(1) / M(0)]$$

where I(1) = Index value at time 1

I(0) = Index value at time 0

M(1) = Aggregate market value at time 1

M(0) = Aggregate market value at time 0

Elimination of price falls at 'ex-dividend' dates is achieved by deducting the dividend amount from M(0).

If no trading price is registered, the previous day's trading price is used, except that a) the present day's bid price is used if this is higher than the previous day's traded price, and b) the present day's offer price is used if this is lower than the previous day's traded price.

New companies or share classes are included from the second day of trading, with the previous market value, i.e. M(0), being corrected through the addition of the company's or share class value from the first day of trading. Delistings involve the same approach with the correction being a subtraction.

In the case of share splits, ordinary issues, bonus issues and dividend issues with preferential rights for existing shareholders, the new shares are included in the weighted calculation base from the 'ex-date'. It is assumed that for ordinary and dividend issues 100% of the issue is subscribed to, with later corrections being made when relevant information is available.

For private placings and for shares issued on mergers, conversions, etc., the issue date is used for the adjustment of the weighted calculation base.

POLAND

Title in Publication

WIG All Shares Index

CONCEPTS AND COVERAGE

Definition

The index is a total return index covering the main section of the Warsaw Stock Exchange.

Coverage

All listed companies are considered in the compilation, but excluding foreign companies and investment funds. The index coverage is extended at the end of each quarter to new companies and to new shares of already existing companies that have been introduced to trading within the quarter.

SOURCE

Source Agencies

The Warsaw Stock Exchange compiles the WIG index.

Key national publication sources

The index is published by the Warsaw Stock Exchange, in the statistical appendix to the monthly Information Bulletin of the National Bank of Poland and by various electronic news services.

Reference period and unit of measurement

The source data are based on 16 April 1991 = 1000. The monthly series shown in the Bank's Bulletin detail both monthly averages and end of month data.

The MEI series are monthly averages of daily data and based on 16 April 1991 = 100

DATA MANIPULATION

Aggregation method and weights

The index is a market weighted index measuring the percentage changes in the market values of shares admitted to trading. The market value of all such companies is computed once a day during each trading session and compared with the value at previous sessions. The price used is the transaction price.

If no non-market changes have occurred in a trading session, the index is calculated through the ratio of the current market capitalisation to that of the previous session. If non-market changes (additional shares through dividend or subscription rights issues, delistings, etc.) have occurred, the index is calculated in relation to the base date capitalisation but with the use of a 'chain index factor' designed to reflect the specific change that has occurred.

Weighting of an individual company is limited to 10%, of an individual sector to 30%, of the total weighting. Reduction to these participation limits is carried out at the time of the quarterly review noted above.

Banking presently has a 30% weight and chemicals some 15%.

PORTUGAL

Title in Publication

BVL General Share Price Index

CONCEPTS AND COVERAGE

Definition

The General Share Price Index of the Bolsa de Valores de Lisboa (BVL) is a price index designed to measure the general level of prices of variablc yield securities (shares) listed on the first section, the 'Market with Official Quotations', of the exchange.

Coverage

Since September 1991 there are three markets: the Market with Official Quotations, the Second Market and the Market without Quotations. The last two are small by comparison with the first and cover shares not qualifying for admission into the first section and trading in scrips and in subscription rights.

The BVL is responsible for trading in shares, while the Oporto Stock Exchange is concerned with the futures market.

The conditions for admission into the first section require that at least 25% of the underwritten share capital or 500,000 shares are publicly spread, that the market capitalisation or the issuer's net worth is above a defined minimum and that the issuer is considered to be in a sound financial position.

Excluded from the index compilation are companies in which other listed companies have holdings above a minimum limit (although for operational reasons this has not been implemented) and companies whose shares are infrequently traded (i.e. not traded for 5 consecutive trading sessions, but with re-entry permissible after trading in two consecutive sessions).

Foreign companies and enterprises affiliated with non-resident companies would be considered for inclusion. By December 1997, however, no such companies had been listed. Enterprises with state participation in their capital are included.

% Weighting and Number of Components

	1990		1996	
	%	No.	%	No.
Food Products and Beverages	4.68	16	2.69	4
Paper Indusry	4.76	3	4.94	3
Non-metallic Mineral Products	1.69	6	4.93	5
Electrical Equipment	3.27	3	0.40	2
Construction	5.21	11	1.14	3
Post and Telecommunications	3.10	1	17.67	2
Finance	50.13	20	38.33	16
Insurance and Pension Funds	3.62	4	5.06	4
Other	23.54	59	24.84	32
Total	100.00	123	100.00	71

SOURCE

Source Agencies

The BVL compiles and publishes the data, which are also published by the Banco de Portugal.

Key national publication sources

The BVL's daily Boletim de Cotações (Quotations Bulletin) and its quarterly Análise de Mercado de Valores Mobiliários (Securities Market Analysis), Tables C4, C5 and C6 for daily index, monthly index and weightings respectively. Additionally the bank's monthly Boletim Estatístico (Statistical Bulletin) presents the general and sector share price indices.

Breakdown available/Other related indices

Seven sectoral indices of the general index have been compiled since January 1991 relating to Food products and beverages; Non-metallic mineral products; Construction; Financial services; Insurance and pension funds; Other business activities; Recreational, cultural and sporting activities.

Published since January 1993 is the BVL 30 index, based on 30 shares of the first section deemed to be most representative from the viewpoint of their liquidity and market capitalisation.

Methodological references

A complete description of the methodology employed is contained in 'Official Stock Market Indexes, Methodology of Construction', published jointly by the BVL and Universidade Católica Portuguesa.

Reference period and unit of measurement

The source index is daily, starting in January 1988 and based on 5 January 1988 = 1000. It is published one day after the reference day. The BVL's related monthly index refers to the end of the month.

The MEI index refers to the average of daily quotations.

DATA MANIPULATION

Aggregation method and weights

Companies included in the index are chosen in order to constitute a basket reflecting the general market climate, in other words reflecting movements in the prices of all shares listed on the Official Quotation Market. It is therefore a portfolio of companies whose capitalisation reflects that of the market. The weighting of each constituent of the index is given by the ratio of its capitalisation to the portfolio's total capitalisation. The index on a specific date is the weighted arithmetic average of the ratios between prices on that date and on a base date. The index is chain-linked between consecutive periods.

Weights are permanently adjusted when changes in the market occur which do not stem from price movements associated with investor expectations. Adjustments to the base are thus made for new companies admitted, for delistings of companies, for changes in the number of outstanding shares of listed companies (excluding non-convertible shares), for capital increases with subscription rights issues or bonus issues at the time when they are announced and when they are reserved for shareholders, for price decreases associated with ex-dividend dates. In this last case, the adjustment is made on the basis of the gross dividend, that is inclusive of tax. Adjustments are not made in respect of bonus issues and capital increases with subscriptions not reserved for shareholders or capital increase by convertible bonds issue.

Formula

The current index is derived as:

$$\text{previous value of index} * \frac{\text{Current value of new portfolio}}{\text{Value at time of adjustment of new portfolio}}$$

SPAIN

Title in Publication

MSE General Index

CONCEPTS AND COVERAGE

Definition

The Madrid Stock Exchange (MSE) General Index refers to spot prices of shares traded on the Madrid exchange, although shares can be negotiated on Spain's four inter-connected exchanges (Madrid, Barcelona, Bilbao and Valencia).

Coverage

The shares included in the index calculation are a sample of all shares traded on the Madrid Stock Exchange. Criteria for the annual sample selection relate to capitalisation, turnover and frequency of transactions. Currently the shares of more than 100 companies are included, representing some 85% of total market capitalisation. Foreign companies are excluded, as are units of investment and mutual funds.

SOURCE

Source Agencies

The Madrid exchange compiles the basic daily index while the Bank of Spain compiles several indices including end of month data.

Key national publication sources

The exchange shows daily indices in its Bulletin and annual series in the statistical appendix to its annual 'Informe del Mercado'. Additionally, there is daily dissemination through the Internet at: //WWW.bolsamadrid.es

The Bank of Spain publishes end of month figures at table 22.23 of its monthly Statistical Bulletin.

% Weighting and Number of Components

	1990		1995	
	%	No.	%	No.
Banks and Financial Institutions	30.87	11	31.65	19
Utilities	14.80	8	21.55	11
Food, Beverages and Tobacco	5.15	8	3.12	12
Construction	13.77	12	7.52	16
Portfolio and Investment	5.88	8	2.91	6
Communication	8.49	4	12.07	6
Iron and Steel Industry	5.91	12	3.64	12
Oil and Chemicals	11.37	9	10.19	10
Other	3.76	3	7.35	15
Total	100.00	75	100.00	107

Breakdown available/Other related series

Several sub-indices are published, daily for the Exchange and end of month for the Bank, including Banks and Financial Institutions; Utilities; Food, Beverages and Tobacco; Construction; Portfolio and Investment; Communication; Iron and Steel; Oil and Chemicals; Other.

The MSE and the Bank also publish the IBEX-35, related to the 35 most traded companies in the interconnected system.

Methodological references

The Madrid exchange published a methodological description of the index in 'Indices de cotization de acciones de la Bolsa de Madrid 1941-1991', which was summarised by the bank in the October 1993 edition of its monthly bulletin.

Reference period and unit of measurement

The source index is based on 31 December 1985 = 100 and is available from January 1985.

The MEI data are averages of daily figures. This series is constructed by the Bank of Spain for inclusion in the MEI publication.

DATA MANIPULATION

Aggregation method and weights

The general index is computed as the aggregation of the nine sector indices, weighted by the ratio of the capitalisation of all shares of the sector (i.e.selected or not) to the capitalisation of all shares listed on the exchange. The sector indices are computed as the aggregation of individual share indices, weighted by the ratio of the capitalisation of the share in the sector to the total capitalisation of all shares representing the sector (i.e. selected) at the end of the previous year.

All capital changes are made at the level of the individual share index through an adjustment to the previous index.

Adjustments are made at the level of each individual share to eliminate the share price fall associated with the time a share goes ex-dividend. An estimate of the share's annual dividend is divided by 365 and at any time during the year, this estimate of the daily value of the dividend is multiplied by the ratio of the number of days since the beginning of the year over days in the year. The result is subtracted from the price of the share.

The prices of actual transactions are used, and in the event of a lack of trading on a given day, the last available traded price is used.

SWEDEN

Title in Publication

The AFGX Index

CONCEPTS AND COVERAGE

Definition

The AFGX (Affarsvarlden's Generalindex) is a capital weighted index, calculated and administered since 1982 by the company 'SIX'.

Coverage

Included in the AFGX are all shares of all companies registered on the Stockholm Stock Exchange 'A' list. Criteria for inclusion in the 'A' list relate to a documented profit-earning capacity; to defined standards of management, financial control, market value and shareholder base; to accessibility by the general public to shares of the company. In this last case, at least 25% of the shares and 10% of the voting rights must be owned by the public. Blocks of 10% or more of the share capital or voting rights are not deemed to be publicly owned.

Shares of foreign companies can be listed on the exchange. Foreign shares already listed on another stock exchange can be accepted on the basis of the rules that apply to their domestic exchange.

The index is a price index as dividends are not assumed to be re-invested.

SOURCE

Source Agency

SIX is the agency responsible for compiling the index of behalf of Affarsvarlden magazine.

Key national publication sources

The AFGX is published in the source magazine (including its website). It is redistributed by Statistics Sweden (monthly figures) in its Monthly Digest of Swedish Statistics and SCB Economic Indicators Part Two. Monthly figures are also available in databases at the Statistics Sweden website.

Breakdown available/ Other related series

The index is sub-divided into Engineering, Forestry, Trade, Building and Real Estate, Shipping, Investment companies (mixed), Investment companies (pure), Banks, Insurance, Other.

Methodological references

A descriptive note from Affarsvarlden's website was provided by Statistics Sweden.

Reference period and unit of measurement

Monthly data are available from 1949, annual from 1901 (by using older indices). The index is now calculated every minute.

Base period is 31 December 1979 = 100.

The series published in the MEI refers to end of month.

DATA MANIPULATION

Aggregation method and weights

The AFGX is a capital weighted index. Capitalisation values are calculated by the multiplication of the numbers of shares with a price, namely the bid price of the most numerous type of share in the company. The weights are re-calculated each day through an adjustment to the index base to accommodate changes in capitalisation.

Prices are not adjusted to eliminate price variations associated with dividend payments.

SWITZERLAND

Title in Publication

The SBS Total Index

CONCEPTS AND COVERAGE

Definition

The SBS (Swiss Bank Corporation) Total Index includes all capital issues traded at the Swiss Stock Exchange. It covers Swiss companies and those of the Principality of Liechtenstein and is exclusive of dividend re-investment.

Coverage

The index relates to a sample of shares (alle wertpapiere mit Eigenkapitalcharakter -- Aktien, Genuss- und Partizipations-scheine) which are traded on the main and Vorborsen sections of the three largest Swiss exchanges, namely Zurich, Basel and Geneva. Although the intent is to have the index reflect all shares traded, the components are reviewed on the last trading day of June and December. Thus new companies are generally admitted at these times. However, new issues of existing companies are included immediately. Issues that are temporarily suspended are maintained in the index calculation using the last traded price. The last traded price is also used for shares when no trading takes place. In other situations, registered transaction prices are used.

Certain restrictions are placed on the foreign ownership of shares.

SOURCE

Source agencies

The SBS compiles the index, which is transmitted to the OECD by the Banque Nationale Suisse.

Key national publication source

Data are available in La Vie Economique, B9.7 Bourse, Indice SBS des actions suisses, and in electronic news services and in newspapers.

Breakdown available/Other related series

Sector and sub-sector indices, Industry (Food, Machinery, Chemicals) and Services (Banks, Insurance, Trade) are published. In addition, there is the SBS 100 (relating to the 100 firms with the highest capitalisation values), as well as indices produced by the Swiss stock exchange.

Methodological references

A descriptive note, 'Der Bankverein-Index der Schweizer Aktien -- Ziel, Definitionen, Berechnungsmethode', was made available by the SBS.

Reference period and unit of measurement

The source index, based on end December 1958 = 100, starts in January 1959.

The MEI series refers to the last trading day of the month.

DATA MANIPULATION

Aggregation methods and weights

The index is computed as an arithmetic Laspeyres, weighted by capitalisation values. A new base and a chaining of the index is performed when capital changes, both increases and decreases, make such adjusments necessary. The computation takes place daily at closing.

TURKEY

Title in Publication

ISE National-100

CONCEPTS AND COVERAGE

Definition

The ISE (Istanbul Stock Exchange) National-100 is compiled from a selection of companies listed in the National Market section of the exchange. It is regarded as the main index of the Turkish stock market.

Coverage

The exchange has four sections, namely the National Market section and three smaller sections (Regional Market, New Companies Market and Watch-List Companies Market). Investment Trusts are listed in the National Market but are excluded from the index calculation.

Constituent companies of the ISE 100 index must fulfil the following pre-requisites:

a) The stock must have been traded on the exchange for at least 60 days.

b) At the end of the evaluation period, the market value of the stock should be ranked among the first 75% of market values.

c) The daily average traded value of the stock, excluding special and block sales, should be ranked among the first 75% of such values.

d) The stock must have been traded on 75% of the trading days of the the previous one year period.

For companies with more than one group of stocks, only one group will be included.

Stocks are then ranked by market values and by traded values. Those with the highest values are selected for inclusion. The composition of the index is adjusted on the first trading day of each quarter.

Prior to 1991 the index was computed on the basis of total market capitalisation of companies. Since January 1991, the index takes into account only the flotation (i.e. the publicly held portion) of each constituent company. The samples chosen account for some 85% of the capitalisation of that portion of the market open to the public.

% Weighting and Number of Components

October 1997

	%	No.
Manufacturing of which:	33.59	66
- Chemicals	7.72	17
- Metal Products and Machinery	8.74	18
Utilities	6.05	3
Trade and Hotels	5.85	10
Transport and Communications	0.88	3
Finance of which:	32.54	18
- Banks	19.32	7
- Holding and Investment Companies	12.22	9
Total	100.00	100

SOURCE

Source agencies

The ISE compiles the index.

Key national publication sources

The series is published in the monthly Main Economic Indicators of the Prime Ministry State Planning Organization.

Breakdown available/Other related series

Also compiled is an all shares index, further divided into three sector indices (Industrials, Services, Financials) and 15 sub-indices. All indices, including the ISE 100, are additionally compiled as return indices.

Methodological references

A descriptive note from the exchange was made available.

Reference period and unit of measurement

The source series starts in January 1986 and was initially based on January 1986 = 100. As from December 1996, this original base has been amended to read 1. The monthly indices produced by the source are end month.

The MEI series is also end month.

DATA MANIPULATION

Aggregation method and weights

The ISE 100 is a market capitalisation weighted index, constructed on the basis of the publicly-held portion of each constituent company. Only registered transaction prices are taken into account in the compilation.

The index is derived as the current market capitalisation over the current divisor, which is adjusted when:

- a constituent company increases capital through a sale of issues to shareholders or to the public;
- a new company is included (reviewed every three months);
- a constituent stock is removed from the index (reviewed every three months);
- the publicly-held portion of constituent stocks changes (reviewed every three months);
- there are mergers and acquisitions;
- there are company splits.

UNITED KINGDOM

Title in Publication

FT-SE-A Non-Financials

CONCEPTS AND COVERAGE

Definition

The FT-SE-A All Share Index, comprising the Financials, Investment Trusts and Non-Financial sectors, is a market weighted price index, designed to represent the performance of companies resident (for tax purposes) and domiciled in the United Kingdom.

Coverage

Included are companies with a capital value greater than 60 million pounds and at least 25% of whose capital is available for investment by the public. Some 900 companies covering 98% of the total market capitalisation are included. In excess of 660 comprise the non-financial index. The selection of the constituent companies is reviewed each quarter but changes are made between reviews following suspensions, mergers, very large new issues, etc.

Ordinary shares are the basis for the calculations. Where a company has more than one quoted line of ordinary shares and each secondary line is worth less than 20% of the total capitalisation of the company, the primary line of shares is adjusted so that the single line of shares represents the full capitalisation of the company. If a secondary line is worth more than 20%, each line of shares is included separately in the index. Warrants to purchase ordinary shares and convertible securities are not included until they are exercised or converted.

SOURCE

Source agencies

The FTSE indices are calculated and distributed by the Financial Times, the London Stock Exchange and the Faculty and Institute of Actuaries. Since 1995 this work has been undertaken by a new joint company - FTSE International. Ultimate responsibility for the design, management and calculation of the FTSE indices rests with the FTSE Actuaries Share Indices Steering Committee.

Key national publication sources

The daily indices are published as monthly averages and end of month levels in ONS Financial Statistics, Table 7.1G Company security prices and yields.

Breakdown available/Other related indices

The Non-Financial Share Index (before 1994 named the FT-500) comprises five main economic group indices, namely resources (re-named in January 1998 from mineral extraction), general industrials (re-named in January 1995 from general manufacturers), consumer goods, services and utilities. A company is allocated to the sub-sector of a sector whose definition most closely describes the nature of its business. Proportion of profits from each industrial area, ascertained in a review of audited annual accounts, determines the classification of diversified companies.

As the economy's industrial base evolves, reviews of sector breakouts become necessary. The present breakout results from a 1991 review and reflects the growth of the service sector, privatisation of utilities and the relative decline of the UK's basic industries and capital goods manufacturers. Its recommendations were implemented in January 1994, with the sector indices retrospectively calculated from January 1986. The previous review was undertaken in 1970.

A variety of other price indices is available, including the FTSE 100, the FTSE 250, the FTSE 350, the FTSE SmallCap, the FTSE Fledging, etc. Additionally there are published total return indices and information on dividend and earning yields.

Methodological references

A full methodological description is available in 'FTSE Actuaries Share Indices - Guide to Calculation Methods' published by the FTSE Actuaries Share Indices Steering Committee. This publication is avail-

able from FTSE International - St. Alphage House - Podium Floor, 2 Fore Street, London EC2Y 5DA.

Reference period and unit of measurement

The source index, presently based on 31 December 1985 = 1000, represents a monthly average of the end of day trading day price index of the non-financial sector as reported daily in the Financial Times since 1962.

The MEI series is an average of daily figures.

DATA MANIPULATION

Aggregation method and weights

The index is an arithmetic weighted index where weights are the market capitalisation of each company (shares-in-issue multiplied by market price, defined as the mid price of the closing best bid and offer). The index value is a number representing the total market value of all companies within the index at a particular time compared to a comparable calculation at a starting point. It is derived by dividing the total market value by a divisor which, to allow the index value to remain comparable over time, is adjusted when capitalisation amendments are made to the constituents of the index. The more frequent corporate actions that require such adjustments are the issue of new shares, a bonus issue (or stock split), a share repurchase. In the last instance the adjustment is made on the announcement of the repurchase and not when the repurchased shares are cancelled.

No adjustment is made in respect to share price changes due to dividend payments. However, information is presented which shows the effect on the price index of the reduction in share prices when shares go ex-dividend. The figure shown is the cumulative total for the year to date, starting with zero at the beginning of the year.

MAIN SALES OUTLETS OF OECD PUBLICATIONS
PRINCIPAUX POINTS DE VENTE DES PUBLICATIONS DE L'OCDE

AUSTRALIA – AUSTRALIE
D.A. Information Services
648 Whitehorse Road, P.O.B 163
Mitcham, Victoria 3132 Tel. (03) 9210.7777
Fax: (03) 9210.7788

AUSTRIA – AUTRICHE
Gerold & Co.
Graben 31
Wien I Tel. (0222) 533.50.14
Fax: (0222) 512.47.31.29

BELGIUM – BELGIQUE
Jean De Lannoy
Avenue du Roi, Koningslaan 202
B-1060 Bruxelles Tel. (02) 538.51.69/538.08.41
Fax: (02) 538.08.41

CANADA
Renouf Publishing Company Ltd.
5369 Canotek Road
Unit 1
Ottawa, Ont. K1J 9J3 Tel. (613) 745.2665
Fax: (613) 745.7660

Stores:
71 1/2 Sparks Street
Ottawa, Ont. K1P 5R1 Tel. (613) 238.8985
Fax: (613) 238.6041

12 Adelaide Street West
Toronto, QN M5H 1L6 Tel. (416) 363.3171
Fax: (416) 363.5963

Les Éditions La Liberté Inc.
3020 Chemin Sainte-Foy
Sainte-Foy, PQ G1X 3V6 Tel. (418) 658.3763
Fax: (418) 658.3763

Federal Publications Inc.
165 University Avenue, Suite 701
Toronto, ON M5H 3B8 Tel. (416) 860.1611
Fax: (416) 860.1608

Les Publications Fédérales
1185 Université
Montréal, QC H3B 3A7 Tel. (514) 954.1633
Fax: (514) 954.1635

CHINA – CHINE
Book Dept., China National Publications
Import and Export Corporation (CNPIEC)
16 Gongti E. Road, Chaoyang District
Beijing 100020 Tel. (10) 6506-6688 Ext. 8402
(10) 6506-3101

CHINESE TAIPEI – TAIPEI CHINOIS
Good Faith Worldwide Int'l. Co. Ltd.
9th Floor, No. 118, Sec. 2
Chung Hsiao E. Road
Taipei Tel. (02) 391.7396/391.7397
Fax: (02) 394.9176

CZECH REPUBLIC – RÉPUBLIQUE TCHÈQUE
National Information Centre
NIS – prodejna
Konviktská 5
Praha 1 – 113 57 Tel. (02) 24.23.09.07
Fax: (02) 24.22.94.33
E-mail: nkposp@dec.niz.cz
Internet: http://www.nis.cz

DENMARK – DANEMARK
Munksgaard Book and Subscription Service
35, Nørre Søgade, P.O. Box 2148
DK-1016 København K Tel. (33) 12.85.70
Fax: (33) 12.93.87

J. H. Schultz Information A/S,
Herstedvang 12,
DK – 2620 Albertslung Tel. 43 63 23 00
Fax: 43 63 19 69
Internet: s-info@inet.uni-c.dk

EGYPT – ÉGYPTE
The Middle East Observer
41 Sherif Street
Cairo Tel. (2) 392.6919
Fax: (2) 360.6804

FINLAND – FINLANDE
Akateeminen Kirjakauppa
Keskuskatu 1, P.O. Box 128
00100 Helsinki

Subscription Services/Agence d'abonnements :
P.O. Box 23
00100 Helsinki Tel. (358) 9.121.4403
Fax: (358) 9.121.4450

***FRANCE**
OECD/OCDE
Mail Orders/Commandes par correspondance :
2, rue André-Pascal
75775 Paris Cedex 16 Tel. 33 (0)1.45.24.82.00
Fax: 33 (0)1.49.10.42.76
Telex: 640048 OCDE
Internet: Compte.PUBSINQ@oecd.org

Orders via Minitel, France only/
Commandes par Minitel, France exclusivement :
36 15 OCDE

OECD Bookshop/Librairie de l'OCDE :
33, rue Octave-Feuillet
75016 Paris Tel. 33 (0)1.45.24.81.81
33 (0)1.45.24.81.67

Dawson
B.P. 40
91121 Palaiseau Cedex Tel. 01.89.10.47.00
Fax: 01.64.54.83.26

Documentation Française
29, quai Voltaire
75007 Paris Tel. 01.40.15.70.00

Economica
49, rue Héricart
75015 Paris Tel. 01.45.78.12.92
Fax: 01.45.75.05.67

Gibert Jeune (Droit-Économie)
6, place Saint-Michel
75006 Paris Tel. 01.43.25.91.19

Librairie du Commerce International
10, avenue d'Iéna
75016 Paris Tel. 01.40.73.34.60

Librairie Dunod
Université Paris-Dauphine
Place du Maréchal-de-Lattre-de-Tassigny
75016 Paris Tel. 01.44.05.40.13

Librairie Lavoisier
11, rue Lavoisier
75008 Paris Tel. 01.42.65.39.95

Librairie des Sciences Politiques
30, rue Saint-Guillaume
75007 Paris Tel. 01.45.48.36.02

P.U.F.
49, boulevard Saint-Michel
75005 Paris Tel. 01.43.25.83.40

Librairie de l'Université
12*a*, rue Nazareth
13100 Aix-en-Provence Tel. 04.42.26.18.08

Documentation Française
165, rue Garibaldi
69003 Lyon Tel. 04.78.63.32.23

Librairie Decitre
29, place Bellecour
69002 Lyon Tel. 04.72.40.54.54

Librairie Sauramps
Le Triangle
34967 Montpellier Cedex 2 Tel. 04.67.58.85.15
Fax: 04.67.58.27.36

A la Sorbonne Actual
23, rue de l'Hôtel-des-Postes
06000 Nice Tel. 04.93.13.77.75
Fax: 04.93.80.75.69

GERMANY – ALLEMAGNE
OECD Bonn Centre
August-Bebel-Allee 6
D-53175 Bonn Tel. (0228) 959.120
Fax: (0228) 959.12.17

GREECE – GRÈCE
Librairie Kauffmann
Stadiou 28
10564 Athens Tel. (01) 32.55.321
Fax: (01) 32.30.320

HONG-KONG
Swindon Book Co. Ltd.
Astoria Bldg. 3F
34 Ashley Road, Tsimshatsui
Kowloon, Hong Kong Tel. 2376.2062
Fax: 2376.0685

HUNGARY – HONGRIE
Euro Info Service
Margitsziget, Európa Ház
1138 Budapest Tel. (1) 111.60.61
Fax: (1) 302.50.35
E-mail: euroinfo@mail.matav.hu
Internet: http://www.euroinfo.hu//index.html

ICELAND – ISLANDE
Mál og Menning
Laugavegi 18, Pósthólf 392
121 Reykjavik Tel. (1) 552.4240
Fax: (1) 562.3523

INDIA – INDE
Oxford Book and Stationery Co.
Scindia House
New Delhi 110001 Tel. (11) 331.5896/5308
Fax: (11) 332.2639
E-mail: oxford.publ@axcess.net.in

17 Park Street
Calcutta 700016 Tel. 240832

INDONESIA – INDONÉSIE
Pdii-Lipi
P.O. Box 4298
Jakarta 12042 Tel. (21) 573.34.67
Fax: (21) 573.34.67

IRELAND – IRLANDE
Government Supplies Agency
Publications Section
4/5 Harcourt Road
Dublin 2 Tel. 661.31.11
Fax: 475.27.60

ISRAEL – ISRAËL
Praedicta
5 Shatner Street
P.O. Box 34030
Jerusalem 91430 Tel. (2) 652.84.90/1/2
Fax: (2) 652.84.93

R.O.Y. International
P.O. Box 13056
Tel Aviv 61130 Tel. (3) 546 1423
Fax: (3) 546 1442
E-mail: royil@netvision.net.il

Palestinian Authority/Middle East:
INDEX Information Services
P.O.B. 19502
Jerusalem Tel. (2) 627.16.34
Fax: (2) 627.12.19

ITALY – ITALIE
Libreria Commissionaria Sansoni
Via Duca di Calabria, 1/1
50125 Firenze Tel. (055) 64.54.15
Fax: (055) 64.12.57
E-mail: licosa@ftbcc.it

Via Bartolini 29
20155 Milano Tel. (02) 36.50.83

Editrice e Libreria Herder
Piazza Montecitorio 120
00186 Roma Tel. 679.46.28
Fax: 678.47.51

Libreria Hoepli
Via Hoepli 5
20121 Milano Tel. (02) 86.54.46
Fax: (02) 805.28.86

Libreria Scientifica
Dott. Lucio de Biasio 'Aeiou'
Via Coronelli, 6
20146 Milano Tel. (02) 48.95.45.52
Fax: (02) 48.95.45.48

JAPAN – JAPON
OECD Tokyo Centre
Landic Akasaka Building
2-3-4 Akasaka, Minato-ku
Tokyo 107 Tel. (81.3) 3586.2016
Fax: (81.3) 3584.7929

KOREA – CORÉE
Kyobo Book Centre Co. Ltd.
P.O. Box 1658, Kwang Hwa Moon
Seoul Tel. 730.78.91
Fax: 735.00.30

MALAYSIA – MALAISIE
University of Malaya Bookshop
University of Malaya
P.O. Box 1127, Jalan Pantai Baru
59700 Kuala Lumpur
Malaysia Tel. 756.5000/756.5425
Fax: 756.3246

MEXICO – MEXIQUE
OECD Mexico Centre
Edificio INFOTEC
Av. San Fernando no. 37
Col. Toriello Guerra
Tlalpan C.P. 14050
Mexico D.F. Tel. (525) 528.10.38
Fax: (525) 606.13.07

E-mail: ocde@rtn.net.mx

NETHERLANDS – PAYS-BAS
SDU Uitgeverij Plantijnstraat
Externe Fondsen
Postbus 20014
2500 EA's-Gravenhage Tel. (070) 37.89.880
Voor bestellingen: Fax: (070) 34.75.778

Subscription Agency/ Agence d'abonnements :
SWETS & ZEITLINGER BV
Heereweg 347B
P.O. Box 830
2160 SZ Lisse Tel. 252.435.111
Fax: 252.415.888

NEW ZEALAND – NOUVELLE-ZÉLANDE
GPLegislation Services
P.O. Box 12418
Thorndon, Wellington Tel. (04) 496.5655
Fax: (04) 496.5698

NORWAY – NORVÈGE
NIC INFO A/S
Ostensjoveien 18
P.O. Box 6512 Etterstad
0606 Oslo Tel. (22) 97.45.00
Fax: (22) 97.45.45

PAKISTAN
Mirza Book Agency
65 Shahrah Quaid-E-Azam
Lahore 54000 Tel. (42) 735.36.01
Fax: (42) 576.37.14

PHILIPPINE – PHILIPPINES
International Booksource Center Inc.
Rm 179/920 Cityland 10 Condo Tower 2
HV dela Costa Ext cor Valero St.
Makati Metro Manila Tel. (632) 817 9676
Fax: (632) 817 1741

POLAND – POLOGNE
Ars Polona
00-950 Warszawa
Krakowskie Prezdmiescie 7 Tel. (22) 264760
Fax: (22) 265334

PORTUGAL
Livraria Portugal
Rua do Carmo 70-74
Apart. 2681
1200 Lisboa Tel. (01) 347.49.82/5
Fax: (01) 347.02.64

SINGAPORE – SINGAPOUR
Ashgate Publishing
Asia Pacific Pte. Ltd
Golden Wheel Building, 04-03
41, Kallang Pudding Road
Singapore 349316 Tel. 741.5166
Fax: 742.9356

SPAIN – ESPAGNE
Mundi-Prensa Libros S.A.
Castelló 37, Apartado 1223
Madrid 28001 Tel. (91) 431.33.99
Fax: (91) 575.39.98

E-mail: mundiprensa@tsai.es
Internet: http://www.mundiprensa.es

Mundi-Prensa Barcelona
Consell de Cent No. 391
08009 – Barcelona Tel. (93) 488.34.92
Fax: (93) 487.76.59

Libreria de la Generalitat
Palau Moja
Rambla dels Estudis, 118
08002 – Barcelona
(Suscripciones) Tel. (93) 318.80.12
(Publicaciones) Tel. (93) 302.67.23
Fax: (93) 412.18.54

SRI LANKA
Centre for Policy Research
c/o Colombo Agencies Ltd.
No. 300-304, Galle Road
Colombo 3 Tel. (1) 574240, 573551-2
Fax: (1) 575394, 510711

SWEDEN – SUÈDE
CE Fritzes AB
S–106 47 Stockholm Tel. (08) 690.90.90
Fax: (08) 20.50.21

For electronic publications only/
Publications électroniques seulement
STATISTICS SWEDEN
Informationsservice
S-115 81 Stockholm Tel. 8 783 5066
Fax: 8 783 4045

Subscription Agency/Agence d'abonnements :
Wennergren-Williams Info AB
P.O. Box 1305
171 25 Solna Tel. (08) 705.97.50
Fax: (08) 27.00.71

Liber distribution
Internatinal organizations
Fagerstagatan 21
S-163 52 Spanga

SWITZERLAND – SUISSE
Maditec S.A. (Books and Periodicals/Livres et périodiques)
Chemin des Palettes 4
Case postale 266
1020 Renens VD 1 Tel. (021) 635.08.65
Fax: (021) 635.07.80

Librairie Payot S.A.
4, place Pépinet
CP 3212
1002 Lausanne Tel. (021) 320.25.11
Fax: (021) 320.25.14

Librairie Unilivres
6, rue de Candolle
1205 Genève Tel. (022) 320.26.23
Fax: (022) 329.73.18

Subscription Agency/Agence d'abonnements :
Dynapresse Marketing S.A.
38, avenue Vibert
1227 Carouge Tel. (022) 308.08.70
Fax: (022) 308.07.99

See also – Voir aussi :
OECD Bonn Centre
August-Bebel-Allee 6
D-53175 Bonn (Germany) Tel. (0228) 959.120
Fax: (0228) 959.12.17

THAILAND – THAÏLANDE
Suksit Siam Co. Ltd.
113, 115 Fuang Nakhon Rd.
Opp. Wat Rajbopith
Bangkok 10200 Tel. (662) 225.9531/2
Fax: (662) 222.5188

TRINIDAD & TOBAGO, CARIBBEAN TRINITÉ-ET-TOBAGO, CARAÏBES
Systematics Studies Limited
9 Watts Street
Curepe
Trinidad & Tobago, W.I. Tel. (1809) 645.3475
Fax: (1809) 662.5654

E-mail: tobe@trinidad.net

TUNISIA – TUNISIE
Grande Librairie Spécialisée
Fendri Ali
Avenue Haffouz Imm El-Intilaka
Bloc B 1 Sfax 3000 Tel. (216-4) 296 855
Fax: (216-4) 298.270

TURKEY – TURQUIE
Kültür Yayinlari Is-Türk Ltd.
Atatürk Bulvari No. 191/Kat 13
06684 Kavaklidere/Ankara
Tel. (312) 428.11.40 Ext. 2458
Fax : (312) 417.24.90

Dolmabahce Cad. No. 29
Besiktas/Istanbul Tel. (212) 260 7188

UNITED KINGDOM – ROYAUME-UNI
The Stationery Office Ltd.
Postal orders only:
P.O. Box 276, London SW8 5DT
Gen. enquiries Tel. (171) 873 0011
Fax: (171) 873 8463

The Stationery Office Ltd.
Postal orders only:
49 High Holborn, London WC1V 6HB

Branches at: Belfast, Birmingham, Bristol, Edinburgh, Manchester

UNITED STATES – ÉTATS-UNIS
OECD Washington Center
2001 L Street N.W., Suite 650
Washington, D.C. 20036-4922 Tel. (202) 785.6323
Fax: (202) 785.0350

Internet: washcont@oecd.org

Subscriptions to OECD periodicals may also be placed through main subscription agencies.

Les abonnements aux publications périodiques de l'OCDE peuvent être souscrits auprès des principales agences d'abonnement.

Orders and inquiries from countries where Distributors have not yet been appointed should be sent to: OECD Publications, 2, rue André-Pascal, 75775 Paris Cedex 16, France.

Les commandes provenant de pays où l'OCDE n'a pas encore désigné de distributeur peuvent être adressées aux Éditions de l'OCDE, 2, rue André-Pascal, 75775 Paris Cedex 16, France.

12-1996

OECD PUBLICATIONS, 2, rue André-Pascal, 75775 PARIS CEDEX 16
PRINTED IN FRANCE
(31 98 14 1 P) ISBN 92-64-16036-1 – No. 49935 1997